INSIDE the
MIND
of the
TURTLES

INSIDE
the
MIND
of the
TURTLES

CURTIS M. FAITH

New York   Chicago   San Francisco   Lisbon   London   Madrid   Mexico City
Milan   New Delhi   San Juan   Seoul   Singapore   Sydney   Toronto

1 2 3 4 5 6 7 8 9 0   /   0 1 0 9

ISBN   978-0-07-160243-3
MHID   0-07-160243-7

McGraw-Hill books are available at special discounts to use as premiums and sales promotions, or for use in corporate training programs. For more information, please write to the Director of Special Sales, Professional Publishing, McGraw-Hill, Two Penn Plaza, New York, NY 10121-2298. Or contact your local bookstore.

This book is printed on acid-free paper.

For Jennifer
my *sine qua non*

CONTENTS

LIFE IN THE SHELL

Behold the turtle. He makes progress only when he sticks his neck out.
—James Bryant Conant

I remember the first time I realized that I had earned a bit of notoriety. I was flying from Reno, Nevada, to the East Coast, and I was sitting next to a man in his mid-50s. We were chatting about our respective backgrounds, and I mentioned I had once been part of a group of commodities traders taught by a famous trader in Chicago. I was shocked when he asked me, "You aren't one of the Turtles, are you?"

I was. Since the mid-1980s, I have been a Turtle, one of a group of commodities traders who were taught by the famous Chicago trader Richard Dennis. Rich was famous for turning a few thousand dollars into a fortune of over $200 million by the time he was 35. Rich and his friend and business partner, William Eckhardt, taught 12 of us to trade in two weeks in December 1983 and then set us loose with Rich's millions. Over the course of the next 4½ years, we earned over $100 million for him, a feat for which we too became famous. As a Turtle, I earned Rich over $30 million dollars, the most of any of the Turtles. This was a story that my fellow traveler obviously had heard.

I told the complete story of my becoming a Turtle in my first book, *Way of the Turtle*, where I explained the psychological basis of market movements that enabled us to make that money as well as many of the techniques we used to trade as Turtles. Our group's success became legend in the world of trading. It was the first time that anyone had definitively demonstrated that trading could be taught. Many new traders were anxious to learn our secrets.

After I retired from trading, once the Turtle program ended, and began my life as an entrepreneur, I was introduced to the world of venture capital and angel investing. There, I noticed that the way many of the best entrepreneurs, venture capitalists, and traders approached risk was actually similar to the way that the Turtles approached risk. We looked at risk not as something to be feared and avoided but as something to be respected and understood, because we knew, as did James Bryant Conant, that we could not make progress without sticking our necks out a bit.

James Bryant Conant was president of Harvard University, a science advisor to President Roosevelt in 1941, and the U.S. government's civilian administrator of the infamous Manhattan Project. In the quote at the beginning of this Preface, Conant referenced the relationship between progress and risk. In this book I explore the role of risk in trading, investing, building new companies, and making life decisions. I also explain how the way people view and manage risk can affect their ability to innovate and move forward.

Many of the lessons learned by the Turtles are applied by venture capitalists and successful entrepreneurs to other, more common circumstances under the umbrella of managing risk in an uncertain world. These lessons are especially important because people are not very good at making decisions when there are no identifiable correct answers or when the risk of failure is significantly high. In fact, people systematically make all sorts of errors when making decisions around uncertainty and risk.

After the Turtle program ended, I became good friends with a former emergency room doctor and found out that the way they approach risk and the uncertainty of diagnosis and patient response was very similar to the approaches used by traders and entrepreneurs.

In this book I will take you inside the mind of the Turtles and others who master risk every day. I will outline the strategies used by the Turtles, professional traders, entrepreneurs, venture capitalists, and emergency room doctors for anticipating, managing, and mitigating risk. I will also show how these strategies can be applied in more common everyday situations. Before I begin my discussion of risk, though, I want to show you just how important making the right decisions under uncertainty can be.

ACKNOWLEDGMENTS

I want to express my thanks to those who helped make this book what it is.

I want to thank those who volunteered their time answering my interview questions: Jerry Parker, Bruce Tizes, Ted Patras, Simon Olson, Niall Gannon, Howard Lindzon, Van Tharp, and Jack Schwager. I also extend my thanks to Brett Steenbarger who graciously allowed me to include some of his material for the chapter on overcoming fear.

My editor Jeanne Glasser, editorial director at McGraw-Hill, kept me writing until this book met her high standards. Thank you, Jeanne, for not accepting anything less than my best.

During the course of editing, Jennifer Jordie, Levi Freedman, and Anthony Garner offered their comments and criticism. Thank you.

Finally, I want to thank everyone at McGraw-Hill who has helped shape the book: Philip Ruppel, president of McGraw-Hill Professional; Maureen Harper, production manager; Daina Penikas, senior editing supervisor; Morgan Ertel, editorial assistant; Gaya Vinay, marketing manager; Lydia Rinaldi, director of publicity; Laura Friedman, senior director of marketing; Keith Pfeffer, senior director of national accounts; Anthony Landi, senior art director and cover designer; Edwin Durbin, indexer; James Madru, copyeditor; Penny Linskey, proofreader; and Scott Rattray, compositor and designer.

Part One

THE SEVEN RULES FOR MANAGING RISK

LIFE, DEATH, AND UNCERTAINTY

Don't waste life in doubts and fears; spend yourself on the work before you,
well assured that the right performance of this hour's duties will be the
best preparation for the hours and ages that will follow it.
—Ralph Waldo Emerson

When I was 23 years old, I faced my first real life-or-death decision. It wasn't my life at stake, but that of my friend Albert.
Albert was about 15 years older than me, a husband and father of two,
and I had only a handful of seconds to make a decision that I knew I
might regret for the rest of my life. I was out of the water, standing on
one of two 5.8-meter-long narrow white pontoons of a Nacra racing
catamaran that lay on its side. I was in no danger myself.

Albert, however, had missed his chance to grab onto the boat, and he
was now 20 or 30 feet away. The wind was so strong that the trampoline, normally only for sitting, was now acting as a sail and moving the
boat faster than Albert could swim. I was moving with it, away from him.

We were three miles from the nearest shore and about two hours
from sunset. While it was the middle of July, sunny, and 80 degrees, the
water was very cold. In the summer, the surface temperature of the water
rose, but as little as four or five feet below the surface the water was only

• 3 •

45 degrees. The huge waves had stirred up the water so that the surface water was mixing with the deeper water and dropping in temperature. I knew that Albert would not live through the night by himself.

Less than a half hour earlier we had left my dock on the shore of Crystal Bay, Nevada, and set out into the windy day. There were whitecaps all across the lake, but this normally meant great sailing. I liked whitecaps. The dock was in the wind shadow of the southern-pointing peninsula of land dividing Crystal Bay from the larger portion of northern Lake Tahoe. The prevailing winds came from the southeast, so the peninsula blocked both the wind and the waves; it also hid the dangers of this freak summer storm.

Within two or three minutes of leaving the dock it was clear that the wind and the waves were not like anything I had seen before. My catamaran had two trapeze wires; these wires and the harnesses we both wore around our waists allowed us to counter the force of the wind by moving our bodies out over the water. When the wind was really strong, we would have both feet planted on the side of the hull, increasing the leverage of our weight, helping to keep the catamaran upright. Albert and I were both big guys, so we would normally have no trouble keeping the Nacra upright.

This day was different. The waves were huge. The swells were easily 12 to 15 feet, so we could see the shore only when riding the crests. As we dropped into the troughs, we could only see our boat and the waves. This is not uncommon on the open ocean, but I had never seen anything like it on Lake Tahoe (which is only 27 miles long). I let the main sheet out as far as it would go to reduce the power of the large main sail, and we were still sailing much faster than I wanted. We were hitting the waves too fast and too hard. Our weight was too far forward, so as we skimmed over the crest of each bank of swells, we would speed up to almost 25 miles per hour and hit the face of the oncoming swell.

The tips of the pontoons, which normally would float over the water, were sinking into it, slowing us down suddenly as they hit the steep face of the next wave. We were in danger of pitch-poling (flipping the boat violently end over end) unless we could get our weight back. The waves were so high I didn't think we could safely turn around and head back to the dock. So I decided instead to head for Sand Harbor, a straight shot across the bay. The waves would be easier to manage if we hit them diagonally.

Albert was still too far forward, adding to the pontoon's tendency to dig into the water. After one sudden slowdown that caused the back of the boat to rise three or four feet into the air, I warned him, "Albert, you need to move back. If we don't get more weight back, we are going to flip the boat." He was scared and unable to move. I couldn't blame him. It was his first time sailing on a catamaran, and the conditions were dangerous. I had been sailing for years, and even I was frightened. I can only imagine what was going through his head. I never should have brought a novice out in these conditions—we were in over our heads, and it was my fault.

We sailed about halfway across the bay when we finally pitchpoled. The inertia of my body kept me moving as the boat crashed into the wave. It stopped, and we didn't. I slammed into Albert, who was ahead of me, knocking his feet from the boat, and we both swung violently into the water while still hanging from the trapeze cables. When I emerged, I could see Albert next to the now capsized boat; I swam toward him.

Within seconds, the wind caught the top of the upside-down trampoline and started to blow the boat onto its side. I found the aluminum mast and was surprised; it was moving rapidly, and I could not grip its smooth surface with my wet hands. I tried again and realized that the boat was moving so fast that I was almost halfway up its 38-foot mast. I knew I had only a few more seconds before it slipped entirely past me. As the end of the mast neared, I reached across to grab the edge of the sail. I hoped that I would be able to get a firm grip on its rough fabric. Making one final grab, I managed to pull myself onto the sail and toward the pontoons. I expected to find Albert waiting on them. He had been much closer to the boat.

He wasn't there.

I turned around, and my heart sunk. Albert was five or six feet beyond the end of the mast. There was no way to reach him. The lines were still attached to the boat, and Albert was too far away already, and each second increased the distance by a foot or more. Too late, I remembered there was one more thing I had neglected to tell my friend Albert.

In sailing, the cardinal rule is stay with the boat. *Always stay with the boat.*

You can climb on top of it to save your strength and keep out of cold water. It will make you more visible to anyone attempting a rescue, much more so than a being a single swimmer in the water, lost among the whitecaps. I pulled one of the five-foot centerboards out of the still-sideways hull and threw it as far as I could toward Albert. I thought he might be able to use it to help stay afloat. The more he could keep his body out of the cold water, the longer he would survive. Taking the other one out, I tossed it as well.

As the wind whipped the whitecaps and blew me further from Albert, I ran through my options. I could stay with him, and in two or three hours we would both be alone, miles from shore, and no one would know where we were as the Nacra hit the beach. Anyone seeing the boat might reasonably assume it had merely broken from a mooring and drifted across the lake. So, if I stayed with Albert, we would most likely both die of exposure during the night.

What if I stayed with the boat? The Nacra 5.8 is a two-person boat. I had capsized it many times, and it was fairly easy to right under normal circumstances using the weight of two people to lift the sail and mast out of the water.

This was different. Being only one person in huge waves, I doubted I could get it up by myself. But I could stay with the boat, try to right it, and sail to shore for help. Even if I could not get the boat sailing, I knew that it was moving faster toward the beach than either of us could swim. I knew that Albert's life depended on my taking decisive action.

In retrospect, I did get some things right. I had made Albert put on a short wetsuit and water-ski-type life vest before we left the dock. Now I knew he would have less trouble staying afloat, and the extra warmth provided by the wetsuit would buy him an extra hour or two before hypothermia kicked in. So we had some time—just not enough daylight left.

You might think that staying with the boat was the easy decision, that I wasn't putting myself in danger by deciding to try to sail for help. I can only tell you that I really didn't want to leave Albert. It was not easy to watch him move further and further away. I wanted to stay with him. As he drifted away slowly, I had the terrible thought I might not see him alive again.

After he left my sight, I tried to right the boat. I knew that Albert's best hope lie in my ability to sail to shore. I was being blown directly onto the beach, so I knew I was safe; in the worst case, I would likely blow ashore to the relatively flat, sandy shore of Incline Village in three or four hours. But Albert didn't have three or four hours. If the sun set while he was still in the water, it would be almost impossible for anyone to find him at night. He would not live until morning in such cold water.

I was expecting it to be very difficult to get the boat upright because under normal circumstances one person did not have enough weight to pull up wet sails. In the past, I had only ever attempted righting the boat with two people, so I was quite surprised that on my first attempt the Nacra came easily out of the water. The large swells helped the tip of the sail to emerge from the water, and the tip of the sail, in turn, caught some wind and continued to pull the sail upward.

However, this caused another problem. The Nacra almost immediately capsized again after I got it upright. Then I had to swim around the boat, being very careful not to lose my grip, to once again right the boat. After about four unsuccessful attempts, I decided to detach the main sheet—the rope that attaches to the back of the large main sail to control its power—figuring that would lessen the tendency to capsize. On my next attempt, the boat stayed upright. Even though the main sheet was unattached, there was still considerable power, and the boat was now moving very fast.

I was now faced with my second important decision: Did I attempt to go back to find Albert myself, or did I sail directly to shore to get help? I was single-handedly sailing a boat designed for two-handed sailing. I was also sailing in the worst conditions I had ever seen on Lake Tahoe. I had lost sight of my friend when he was at most 150 feet away because of the whitecaps and huge swells, so I thought it would be very difficult to find him by boat. I was two miles from land in three different directions, so there was no easy landmark to find my way back. I decided to go directly for help, opting to sail straight downwind because that would be the fastest and easiest point of sail and would take me to a landing where there would be houses and people and help.

Lake Tahoe had a Coast Guard station about six miles away with a rescue plane that could serve to guide rescuers to Albert very quickly. If I could get to shore in time, I thought he had a good chance. I sailed to about three-quarters of a mile from shore, capsizing every five minutes or so. The jib—the smaller sail on the front of the boat—was shredded by the high winds. The main sail also had started to tear. After about four capsizes, it was so destroyed that I could no longer get the boat upright. I was still pretty far from shore but moving rapidly because the wind was still blowing me toward shore much faster than I could swim. All I could do was wait.

After perhaps 30 to 40 minutes, I came close enough to shore that a homeowner on the beach noticed my boat. When I got within shouting distance, I asked her to call the Coast Guard because my friend was still in the water. I told her Albert's estimated position, and she called immediately. (I later found out that the homeowner who so kindly helped me was Dorothy Bridges, wife of the actor Lloyd Bridges and the mother of the actors Beau and Jeff Bridges.) When I finally landed, I called Albert's wife and told her that Albert was still in the lake and that the Coast Guard was on the way to rescue him. She was understandably very upset.

When we saw the Coast Guard plane overhead, those of us who had been waiting onshore became hopeful. Soon thereafter, we heard over the phone that Albert had been spotted. The white dagger board that I had thrown him had been seen from the air. In a little while we received word that Albert was in the rescue boat and on his way back to shore. We cheered and cried, but he was still in danger. He had severe hypothermia and could die of cardiac arrest at any time. His body temperature had dropped into the high 80s. He would not be out of the woods for several more hours.

Albert survived, but neither of us ever forgot that day.

Decisions Under Uncertainty

The two decisions I made that day that affected Albert's chances for living were, *first*, whether or not to leave him and try to get the boat sailing by myself and, *second,* whether or not to sail for Albert or to sail directly for help. These were decisions without known outcomes. I could have decided to stay with Albert; we might have survived, or we both might have died. I could have sailed to try to find Albert, and I might have found him quickly. I also might not have found him, lost precious minutes or hours in the process, and he might have died. It is also possible that I could have done exactly what I did, and he still might have died.

Each of these decisions carried considerable risk, and the consequences were deadly serious. When I made each one, I chose the route that I believed would most likely lead to Albert's successful rescue. I did not hesitate, even though I knew that he very well could die anyway. I remain convinced that my training as a Turtle helped save Albert that day. I was trained to make just these types of decisions under uncertainty. Ones where you could make the "right" decision and things might still turn out badly or where you could make the "wrong" decision and things could still turn out well.

In general, we human beings are not very good at making these types of decisions. In fact, we tend to consistently make the wrong decisions when facing an uncertain situation. In this book I will outline many of the lessons about risk and uncertainty that I learned as a Turtle and subsequently as an entrepreneur. These lessons are equally applicable to decisions in life, business, and government. In fact, the older I get and the more I see of the world, the more apparent it becomes that our collective societal inability to deal with uncertainty in a rational manner is one of the leading causes of waste, delay, and poor resource allocation. In the next two chapters I explain exactly what I mean by risk and uncertainty.

RISK: FRIEND OR FOE?

Don't be afraid to go out on a limb. That's where the fruit is.
—H. Jackson Browne, Jr.

Imagine this scene: nighttime on the banks of the Cunene River on the border between Namibia and Angola in Sub-Saharan Africa. You are camping in a light tent. The camp is dark. The guides are all sleeping. In the distance you hear the rustle of birds taking flight. Suddenly there is a loud crack from a large branch snapping. You open your eyes, now wide awake, and wonder what could be moving so close to your camp. Could it be one of the lions you've seen several times on your journey?

It could be, but probably isn't. But the branch snapping triggered the release of adrenaline—by your sympathetic nervous system. Your adrenaline goes to work making sure that you are alert and ready for action. You won't be getting any sleep anytime soon.

····················· 🐢 ·····················

Most of us are afraid of risk because of the unknown dangers we associate with it. This emotional, gut reaction comes from the same system that wakes us in the bush when we hear something unexpected. The unknown once meant the potential for death or painful dismemberment with lifelong consequences. People fear risk for the same reasons.

Its yet unnamed dangers trigger a sophisticated biological mechanism that runs rampant when faced with new territory or times of chaos. These mechanisms and the psychological responses to uncertainty that had their place in primitive times are now something of a hindrance. Sometimes people avoid risk at all costs, taking the *safe* route, whether in education, career, or personal decisions, shunning high-risk choices in favor of conservative ones.

Yet many people find that even after living a life that is safe and conservative, all too often they are confronted with unintended personal circumstances that present the very same dangers they worked so hard to avoid. The point is that you can't avoid risk—and you can't accurately predict the outcome of every investment, business, or personal decision. Nobody can make predictions with 100 percent accuracy, not even the purported financial experts—economists. I have a few favorite quotes concerning economists that highlight their inability to make accurate predictions:

> *An economist is an expert who will know tomorrow why the things he predicted yesterday didn't happen today.*
>
> —Laurence J. Peter

> *An economist's guess is liable to be as good as anybody else's.*
>
> —Will Rogers

> *Ask five economists and you'll get five different answers—six if one went to Harvard.*
>
> —Edgar R. Fiedler

If the so-called experts can't reliably predict the future in matters of finance and the economy, how can the rest of us hope to cope with uncertainty? In addition to the challenge of uncertainty, people are hampered by the need to make the *right* decision, behaving as if there is only one correct way to go.

The truth is, in complex systems, there is no single right answer or choice. At times, the best you can do is to make an educated guess — even if it results in an undesired outcome. Let's look at exactly what is meant by *risk*.

Risk is defined as "exposure to the consequences of uncertainty." This definition suggests that risk is comprised of three separate components:

1. **Uncertainty** — unknown or unpredictable events or environments.
2. **Consequences** — a change in a market, business environment, or social context.
3. **Exposure** — a financial or social stake in a given outcome.

Let's examine these concepts further. According to this definition, risk only exists if there is exposure to the consequences of the uncertainty that underlies the risk. If you don't have money in the stock market, for example, then you have no exposure to the risk associated with a drop in stock prices — unless, of course, the drop is so significant that it affects other aspects of the economy. If you don't live in a particular country or have any investments there, you don't have any exposure to the risk of an economic meltdown in that country — unless, of course, the meltdown is so severe or the country is so important that its economic problems spread to places where you do have investments.

Uncertainty drives risk. If we knew how to reliably determine future developments, we could always decide whether or not to take a given risk simply by evaluating its potential fallout. If the outcome were predictable or certain, there would be no risk.

In some cases, however, we don't have enough information to make the "correct" decision. At other times, no matter how much research we do or how much we study any number of alternative outcomes, there are too many complicating factors for us to reliably predict future events. We can't predict the weather more than a week into the future. We can't predict the fluctuations in our economy. We can't predict the price of oil. We can't predict the strength of the dollar. We can't predict the strength of the housing market. We can't predict the price of the S&P 500 Index two months out.

This illustrates the two different types of uncertainty:

1. **Informational uncertainty**—uncertainty caused by a lack of information.

2. **Chaotic uncertainty**—uncertainty caused by too much complexity.

The first type of uncertainty arises from practical constraints. It may cost too much in time or money to conduct the research or investigation required to reduce the uncertainty. The viability of a certain product in a particular market, for example, might be unknown initially, but after you conduct market research, you can reduce—and perhaps even eliminate—this type of uncertainty. Say, for instance, that you want to determine the market acceptance for a given product's pricing. You could test-market a product on a limited basis, and the results of your tests would either validate or invalidate prior assumptions, effectively diminishing potential uncertainties and risks for the launch of the product. If you don't have the time or resources required for a market test then the informational uncertainty associated with the decision will remain.

Chaotic uncertainty, in contrast, cannot be eliminated by research, study, or investigation. You can't know months ahead of time that a freak storm or disease will wipe out your vineyard's wine harvest. You can't know months ahead of time that a hurricane will destroy New Orleans. There are simply too many variables that can combine in too many possible ways to predict future outcomes with any degree of accuracy in the presence of chaotic uncertainty.

What this reveals is that some — but not all — uncertainty is avoidable. There is no way to remove all the uncertainty associated with most decisions.

Consequences are the effects of uncertainty. Financial consequences are changes in the value of assets or investments. They can manifest in the price of gold going up or down, the real-estate market dropping, a flood destroying your home, or a toughening economic climate, among other ways.

While the prior examples all can bring you varying degrees of financial hardship, there are other types of consequences that are not primarily monetary in nature. If you spend seven years working to become a lawyer, for example, you may have wasted a great deal of effort if you find out after graduation that you don't actually enjoy practicing law. If you are a product manager for an electronics company and you produce a product that no one likes and no one buys, you are exposed to the consequences of the poor performance of your product. You might get demoted, passed over for promotion, or fired.

In an uncertain world, consequences are a given. You will never be able to predict exactly what will happen in the future. You can only take your best guess, and even that often will be wrong. The best way you can cope with consequences as they arise is to look at them not as bad things but as inevitabilities of reality—which is, after all, what they are.

Exposure can be defined as holding a financial or social stake in a given outcome. So if you don't have any stake in a given venture, then you are not *exposed* to its inherent risks either. In most cases, exposure is measured by your potential to gain or lose money. If you buy a house for $200,000 and you own it outright, then you have exposure to risk in the form of local real-estate market fluctuations or the possibility of fire, flood, earthquake, or any other type of natural disaster. If you buy 1,000 shares of Apple stock for $200 per share, then you have exposure to the price fluctuations of that stock. The extent of your financial participation determines the extent of your exposure. In both of the preceding cases, the full amount of your financial exposure would total $200,000 dollars.

Although many people see exposure as a direct consequence of uncertainty and risk—and thus see themselves as incapable of controlling the extent of their exposure—there are ways for people to both increase and decrease their exposure. While consequences generally are unavoidable for the individual, exposure generally is avoidable in part or entirely. You can't stop the stock market from dropping, for example, but you can sell your stocks so that the drop does not affect you.

Or consider the homeowner example. A homeowner is vulnerable to a decrease in the value of his house—his investment—in the event of fire or flood. But that same homeowner can purchase an insurance policy that covers damage to his investment owing to fire and flood. In the long run, most people find the cost of the insurance policy is a small price to pay—and an easy way to reduce exposure—when you consider the hefty financial consequences of damage or destruction to an uninsured house.

Investors, particularly institutional investors, often view volatility and risk as synonymous. They most certainly are not. Volatility is a necessary but not sufficient measure of risk. In other words, volatility is a necessary component of risk assessment, but by itself totally inadequate. There are many other types of risk that don't show up in volatility-based measures. A few of these key risks include:

 a. *Illiquidity risk*

 b. *Credit risk*

 c. *Short volatility risk*

These risks share the characteristic that they may be benign in most environments, but can assume overwhelming influence during sporadic market events. The post-mid-2007 experience is replete with a multitude of examples where these risks, which were barely visible previously, completely dominated markets and prices. Any risk assessment process that fails to include these event-type risks is fatally flawed and incomplete.

—Jack D. Schwager,
managing director and principal of The Fortune
Group, an alternative asset management firm; and
author of the bestselling book *Market Wizards*.

Despite its often-negative connotations, savvy investors know that exposure has its benefits, and they will often intentionally use leverage to increase the exposure of their investments. They do this because the more exposure to fluctuations in price an investment has, the greater is the investment's potential power. Consider the leverage that financial instruments such as futures contracts and margin accounts give investors in the following two examples.

In this first example, an investor has $4,500 she wants to invest in gold. With gold priced at $900 per ounce, she can buy 5 ounces of gold for $4,500 from a metals broker. If the investor wants to increase the earning potential of her investment, however, she can instead opt to use her $4,500 to purchase a 100-ounce gold futures contract on the Comex metals exchange. This futures contract will allow her to control $90,000 in gold, and the leverage on that contract will be set at 20:1 because every dollar she invests in the futures contract is liable to $20 of exposure. On the one hand, every dollar increase in the price of gold will give the investor a return of $20 to every $1 invested. On the other hand, a relatively small 5 percent drop in price of $45 per ounce would result in a loss of her entire $4,500. Futures contracts have inherent leverage because they allow a relatively small initial investment to control a large amount of an underlying good or commodity.

In this second example, an investor wants to immediately purchase as many shares of Apple stock from his brokerage firm as possible. He knows that if he uses a financial instrument called a *margin account*, he can buy more stock than he otherwise would be able to afford. At a 2:1 margin, a limit set by the U.S. government, every dollar the investor places in the margin account will allow him to purchase up to $2 of stock because his margin account effectively acts as a loan from his brokerage firm to purchase additional shares of stock.

Using his margin account, the investor's $200,000 investment can now buy him 2,000 shares of Apple stock at $200 per share—double the amount of the 1,000 shares he would be able to buy in a normal account. But while his margin account increased the investor's share control of Apple stock, it also increased his exposure. By way of example, if the investor had used a normal account to purchase his stock, a theoretical price drop of Apple stock from $200 to $100 would have lost him $100,000. But because he used a margin account to buy 2,000 shares, then that same theoretical price drop will cause him to lose $200,000 — twice as much as when using a normal account.

As the preceding two examples demonstrate, leverage is a two-edged sword. It increases the potential for profits and losses at the same time because it increases an investment's exposure to the consequences of uncertainty.

Embracing Risk

Many people share the view that risk is bad. As they see it, risk should be avoided — even shunned.

I don't.

I like risk. I embrace risk.

If your goal is to make small, incremental improvements, then you don't need to play with risk. If you want to make giant leaps forward, you cannot avoid it.

If you are content to learn slowly, you can evade most risk. If you want to learn quickly, you must push yourself and risk failure along the way.

While you can make it through much of life without ever taking a seriously risky step, the riskless course is not always the best one. In fact, as this book will show you, when equipped appropriately, even the most risk-averse person can embrace and profit from risk. Armed with the strategies with which this book provides you, you will be able to approach risk more effectively by controlling it, managing it, and mitigating it. And after you've finished reading, you might just be surprised at how much risk you are willing to invite into your life.

UNCERTAINTY

For my part I know nothing with any certainty, but the
sight of the stars makes me dream.
—Vincent van Gogh

U ncertainty is the underlying force driving risk. If you were somehow able to neutralize the element of doubt in a given situation, you could always eliminate your exposure to risk by making a decision that is consistent with the outcome you desire. You could make the best decision because there *would be* a best decision. But the reality of uncertainty negates the possibility of a singular "best decision."

Most often, uncertainty can't be eliminated. Often, people just don't have ample enough resources or time to make more than an educated guess as to what the future might bring. But even if you do happen to have all the time and background information in the world, it is impossible to make perfect decisions. There will always be events you can't predict, competitors you don't yet see, and complicating factors that you can't anticipate. No matter how much information you might have, nor how large and powerful your computer is, nor how sophisticated science has become, nor how much you might study the alternatives, there are too many events and extenuating circumstances that are not predictable with any degree of reliability more than a few days or weeks into the future.

> *I believe the biggest misconception about risk and uncertainty is that people still believe you can invest without risk and uncertainty. Black swans, recessions, and bear markets are common occurrences throughout history and will continue to be. Its strange how many investment professionals and the investing public act surprised when they happen. There is a century of American economic history available for all to study. Wars, recessions, assassinations, bear markets, bank failures, etc. were not one time events. Trying to build a portfolio in the land of milk and honey is a quick ticket to the poor house.*
>
> —**Niall Gannon**,
> director of wealth management and lead member of
> the Gannon Group at Smith Barney, an asset
> manager for ultra-high net worth individuals

As discussed in Chapter 2, uncertainty generally can be sorted into one of the following two categories:

1. **Informational uncertainty**—uncertainty that arises because you lack the necessary time or sufficient resources to explore all the potential outcomes of a situation to the degree required to eliminate uncertainty.

2. **Chaotic uncertainty**—uncertainty that comes from the complexity of a system because there are too many unknowns, too many interacting factors, or too many independent participants.

It is important to note that each type of uncertainty has its own unique effects on a person's psyche, as evidenced by the fact that humans make decisions differently in the presence of chaotic uncertainty than they do in the presence of informational uncertainty. As such, if you want to improve your ability to cope with and respond to risk, which is driven by uncertainty, you must first learn to differentiate between your psychological reactions to chaotic and informational uncertainty.

Chaotic uncertainty is uncertainty that exists within a system over which you have little to no control. The weather is perhaps the most chaotically uncertain system that humans face on a day-to-day basis. No matter what meteorologists do, they have no way of predicting floods, hurricanes, droughts, and blizzards more than a week or two in advance with any real degree of accuracy. Weather forecasters cannot even predict the path of a hurricane with 100 percent accuracy in as short a timeframe as an hour or so into the future. There are too many uncontrollable forces acting simultaneously to make an absolutely fail-proof prediction.

Financial markets operate in much the same way. There are simply too many different players with too many different agendas to enable any one person to reliably predict future prices with anything approaching 100 percent accuracy.

When most people are faced with making important decisions in the face of chaotic uncertainty, their gut reaction is to consult with experts. You've probably found yourself in a similar situation. Even though you know that it's impossible to foresee what the future will bring, your desire to know the inherently unknowable most likely led you to consult experts on the topic. You may even have asked them to predict the future for you. You are by no means alone. If you were, how

A large majority of investors make risk judgments based solely on a manager's track record. This may sound reasonable, but it is in fact a huge mistake. Why? Because the track record may not include events to which the manager's approach is vulnerable. When such events occur in the future, losses can easily be 5 or even 10 times the historical worst loss. This error is due to the history of the track record being incomplete and unrepresentative of a reasonable range of future conditions.

—Jack D. Schwager,
managing director and principal of The Fortune
Group, an alternative asset management firm; and
author of the bestselling book *Market Wizards*

else could you explain the prevalence of "experts" on a wide array of topics on television programming?

Financial television in particular parades a seemingly never-ending display of panels made up of experts with their predictions about particular stocks and the markets. It will go down. It will go up.

[A common misconception is that] previous draw downs are indicative of future draw downs. Not true. Things can be much worse.

—Jerry Parker,
a fellow Turtle and the CEO of Chesapeake Capital,
a managed futures asset manager with over $1 billion
under management

But the truth is . . . the experts are guessing. They don't really know as much as they claim to be able to know. In fact, no one does.

Many people took the advice of the financial "experts" to their great peril as they turned out to be very wrong about the real estate market and very wrong about the stock market over the last several years. Most "experts," including the heads of the government institutions that control the economy were completely wrong about the depth and severity of the financial crisis.

Whereas chaotic uncertainty is nearly impossible to control, there may well be a "correct" or "right" decision for risks involving informational uncertainty, but informational uncertainty is entangled in its own set of complications. Despite the fact that the right decision is theoretically knowable with informational uncertainty, many times the amount of time and resources that must be expended to arrive at that right decision is not justifiable. In this respect, you're not better off facing informational uncertainty as you are chaotic certainty. In both cases, you can't know what the future will bring when you have to make a decision. In essence, uncertainty cannot be eliminated, and you are stuck making imperfect decisions.

So in business, government, and your personal life, you often will make decisions that turn out poorly. You will expose yourself to negative consequences because of those decisions. You will suffer from those decisions.

This problem has accelerated in recent years as competitive product cycles are getting shorter and shorter. Decisions that once could be made in years now must often be made in months or weeks, putting greater and greater pressure on the decision-making process.

Fortunately, however, you can make better decisions and quicker decisions if you understand how to deal with the possibility that your decisions might turn out to be wrong. As the next sections will demonstrate, there are many strategies at your disposal when you find yourself face-to-face with uncertainty.

In circumstances where uncertainty can mean possible danger, people often find themselves reverting to more primitive ways of thinking—to their savage minds. This is most true when they must make decisions that could mean loss or injury.

Evolutionarily speaking, this is not altogether surprising. For primitive humans, the decision to avoid risk as much as possible was a wise one. After all, the risks that they encountered—from extensive blood loss to infection and poisoning to confrontations with lions, bears, and other wildlife—were often too great to surmount. In the best-case scenario, risk-taking was almost certain to bring injury and damage—and in the worst case, it would bring death. When compared with the relatively small cost of avoiding danger, risk-taking was just plain bad sense. The world of the primitive human was one where decisions were more black and white: Avoid the lion or not, avoid the bear or not, avoid the cobra or not. In general, since the risks were so high, a partial strategy did not make sense. If something might kill you, it really made sense to do everything possible to avoid it.

No matter whether you attribute primitive humans' risk aversion to an evolutionary process of natural selection or to human instincts that have been genetically imprinted, the end reality is the same: Savage humans were fearful of danger and avoided risk whenever possible. To err on the side of caution was good strategy. As time progressed and civilization developed from small villages to vast networks of nations that began trading and interacting in sophisticated ways, however, the savage mind of humans started to become a hindrance to them. As we have developed insurance, futures markets, and pools of capital and resources in the form of corporations, and as our risks have diverged from the physiological and veered mainly toward the financial, the very traits and capabilities that served our prehistoric ancestors so well have become modern-day liabilities. As our competition has become focused on money and the power that is derived from it, our savage minds hinder progress. They can cause us to do the wrong thing.

The best strategy for dealing with uncertainty is accepting that biology is by no means destiny. You are not trapped by the inclinations of the savage mind. In fact, you *must* break free of this mind-set if you want to navigate uncertainty more effectively and embrace the reality that there is an unknown aspect to your decision making and to the outcomes of your actions.

The greatest failures in government, business, and life in general come as a direct result of the unrealistic strategies used to deal with uncertainty. So often people and the organizations they run are solely focused on getting the *right* answer, arriving at the *best* solution, or taking the *proper* course. But their energy and efforts are ultimately wasted because they refuse to accept the reality that *right answers do not always exist*, that there often is *no best solution*, and that the *proper course is often obvious only in retrospect*.

You can always pretend that right answers exist, and if you aren't able to arrive at those solutions yourself, there will always be "experts" and pundits to consult with as you attempt to arrive at the single "best" solution. But you will be better off realizing that there are no such things as unconditionally correct answers. So deal with this reality by preparing yourself for the chance you'll be wrong.

What I'm proposing is really quite simple. If you don't know for certain that things will turn out as you expect they will, then you should plan for the possibility that you will be wrong. Don't pretend that your decision was correct after events indicate otherwise. Instead, *seek the truth about your situation* and *continually track its status*. Don't put all your resources into implementing the "right" plan. Instead, *keep some in reserve in case your original plan doesn't work out*. And don't wait to be surprised by the failure of your original plan. Instead, *actively seek evidence that your original plan was off the mark before any indications to the contrary arise*.

Now, I realize that this might appear a bit obvious to many of you. *Of course* you should allow for the possibility of being wrong when you don't know what the future will bring. *Of course* you shouldn't put all your resource eggs into the one "correct" basket.

Except . . . the truth is that most people rarely act in the way they rationally know is best. Just look at the way most government- and large company-sponsored projects are run. These projects are almost always characterized by a winner-takes-all attitude. But when projects are awarded to the winning bidder, to the extent that there is any uncertainty associated with the technology or ideas behind the winning bid, there is exposure to the consequences of that uncertainty. If the technology or the ideas do not live up to their promise, the project could fail, and a lot of time and money potentially could be wasted. And in the case of government-sponsored projects that fall through, the money that is wasted comes out of taxpayers' pockets.

Fortunately, *there is much that you and I can learn from those who deal with uncertainty on a daily basis*. I stopped trading in the late 1980s and moved on to other ventures, such as starting a software company and cofounding a few other companies. After I had enjoyed a few successes and suffered a few failures in my new line of work, I started to note that the most successful entrepreneurs and angel investors approached risk in much the same way that my colleagues in trading and I did. This led me to consider that perhaps the principles I had acquired as a trader coping with market uncertainty had a broader application. "Maybe," I thought, "a person could be taught to effectively cope with uncertainty and risk."

What was at first a passing thought was reaffirmed when, in early 2001, I met Bruce Tizes. Bruce is both a successful trader and a real-estate investor, but his full-time occupation was once as an emergency room doctor at Mount Sinai Hospital in Chicago. It didn't take me long to understand why Bruce was so effective in all three fields. After learning a bit about emergency medicine from him, I discovered that it shares many characteristics with trading and entrepreneurship.

In each of these fields—trading, entrepreneurship, and emergency medicine—the most common workplace crises involve a combination of uncertainty, limited resources, and the need to make decisions quickly and efficiently. For this reason, it logically follows that the best traders, entrepreneurs, and emergency room doctors have developed similar strategies for dealing with their occupational hazards, if you will—namely, risk and uncertainty. I call the experts who have learned how to manage risk, the *masters of risk*, and in Chapter 4 I will introduce the strategies they share for effectively managing risk and uncertainty.

four

LEARNING FROM THE MASTERS OF RISK

Our main business is not to see what lies dimly at a distance,
but to do what lies clearly at hand.
—Thomas Carlyle

I remember the very first trade I made. My first trading mentor, Rotchy Barker, had generously let me stay in his family's summer house on Lake Geneva in Wisconsin, where many of the best traders from Chicago had summer homes. Rotchy had to leave to go back to his home in Illinois before the markets closed, and he left me to watch a small position of five S&P 500 contracts. I was given instructions to sell them if they dropped below a certain price.

I can still feel the adrenaline of panic when the price moved to the point where he told me to get out. I had to do something quickly that I had never done before. I had to call and place a trade. If I screwed up, I might cost Rotchy quite a sum of money and lose his trust.

I called the number that Rotchy had left and placed an order to get out at a certain price, trying my very best to emulate the wording that Rotchy had used when he placed his own orders. When the price dropped further and I had not received a call confirming that my order had been completed, I worried. I thought Rotchy might be mad the next day when he found out that I botched the order. I moved the price for the order a bit lower, and when I received a call that the order had been filled, I was thoroughly relieved.

That was my baptism into the brotherhood of uncertainty. It was extraordinarily nerve-wracking not knowing what would happen, having to wait to see what the markets did. When I placed the order, there was no way to know whether or not the price would go up or down, no way to know if my order would be filled or not, no way to know exactly how to place the trade. There was no "right" answer. No way to predict.

Uncertainty and the risk stemming from it are at the very core of trading. *Without risk, there would be no potential for profit.* Traders take on risk in exchange for the potential for making money. That is their function. The ones who do this well make money. The ones who do this poorly lose money. This is the essence of the game.

Good traders approach risk the same way that good surfers approach the ocean waves they ride. Timing and judgment are paramount. First, you need to choose the right wave. Choose one too big, and you'll and up getting smashed as the wave curls over too quickly and smashes you with tons of water. Choose one too small, and you will cost yourself the opportunity to ride a great wave. Second, you need to time your drop-in—also known as the start—perfectly. If you go early, you will get smashed, and if you go late, the wave will pass you by without moving you forward.

For traders, the markets present the same sorts of opportunities that waves present for surfers. Not every potential trade should be taken, just as not every wave should be attacked. There are no sure things, but there are trades where the odds tip in your favor. These are the trades that should be taken. Now there is a lot of skill and specific expertise involved in knowing exactly when the odds tip into the trader's favor, but surprisingly, those skills are not what distinguishes the great traders from the losers or even from the adequate traders.

What distinguishes the great from the adequate is how well they deal with risk and uncertainty, how well they handle the difficulty of not knowing what the future will bring. Just as surfers must risk falling and getting slammed by the waves if they are to ride waves, traders must be able to risk losing in order to be able to make money trading. Without risk, there is no reward. The great traders are able to continue trading even when others stop because they understand that it is impossible to predict the future and that losing is part of trading.

For the great traders, risk is part of the landscape—the high mountains that need to be traversed to get to the promised riches on the other side. Great traders know that they must slog their way up the hills; they must do the hard work of losing when a trade inevitably goes wrong in order to be in a position to win when the good trades emerge. At the same time, great traders know that risk needs to be carefully controlled or it can be lethal. Much like medicine that can help in small doses but will kill when taken in larger quantities, risk is necessary but dangerous. Great traders spend a lot of time and effort managing the risk inherent in their trades.

After I retired from trading, I came to see how many of the same principles I used when trading also applied to taking risks when I started my business. From this experience, I was able to extend those trading principles as well as from my experience as an entrepreneur into general rules for mastery of risk and uncertainty. Here are the seven rules great traders use to manage risk and uncertainty. They can be applied to any area in your professional or personal life. They are

1. **Overcome fear.** Great traders know that fear can choke our decision process and cause us to avoid taking risks. Fear also can paralyze you when you need to act quickly and decisively to save yourself from danger—the deer-in-the-headlights syndrome. All great traders have mastered their fears and are able to act decisively when needed.

2. **Remain flexible.** As a trader, you never know which stock or which market may make a move. This is the essence of uncertainty. You don't know what is going to happen. When you don't know what is going to happen, the best strategy is to be ready for anything.

3. **Take reasoned risks.** Many beginners trade like they are sitting at a Las Vegas craps table. They put too much money at risk, and they trade based on hunches, rumors, or someone else's advice. They take foolish risks. Great traders take reasoned risks. A reasoned risk is more like an educated guess than a roll of the dice. Great traders are not gamblers.

4. **Prepare to be wrong.** If you don't know what the future will bring and you choose a trade that assumes a particular outcome, you are possibly going to be wrong. Depending on the type of trade, in many cases it can even be more likely that you will lose money than that you will win money. What matters in the end is the total money won and lost, not whether you are right more often than wrong. Great traders are comfortable making decisions when they know they could be wrong.

5. **Actively seek reality.** As a trader, nothing is more important than an accurate picture of reality. Traders know that their

decisions will result in losses. They also know that they need to know about these losses as soon as possible. A focus on what the market actually does, the market's reality, keeps successful traders from burying their heads in the sand and pretending that the world is other than it actually is.

6. **Respond quickly to change.** Just as important as actively seeking reality and facing that reality is doing something when that reality is not what you wanted, when the uncertain future brings the unhoped-for. When the market moves to price levels that a trader has previously determined would be the place to get out of a trade—by selling what he bought previously, for example—a competent trader will respond quickly and get out, thereby reducing his exposure to continued uncertainty to zero.

7. **Focus on decisions, not outcomes.** One of the reasons that great traders can so easily reverse course is that they have a more sophisticated view of the meaning of error for decisions made under uncertainty. They understand that the fact that things did not turn out the way they had hoped does not necessarily mean that taking the trade was a mistake. They know that many times good ideas don't work out. The very presence of uncertainty ensures that you will be wrong some of the time. All great traders put trades on for a particular reason, and they take them off for a particular reason too. Great traders focus on the reasons for the trades instead of the outcomes for a few given trades.

In the rest of this chapter I'll further outline how each rule applies to trading. Later in the book I will dedicate a full chapter to discussing each rule as it applies to all areas of life in greater detail.

> *Though I wouldn't consider myself a "trader" in the classical sense, Curtis has assembled a list of rules that would benefit long-term investors as well as traders. Whether the holding period is ten minutes or ten years this list is heavy on self-evaluation, criticism, and humility. These traits help ensure that your mistakes are minimized while trying to maximize your value proposition in the markets.*
>
> —Niall Gannon

Overcome Fear

Fear can be both a help and a hindrance in life. Fear causes us to avoid danger. But great traders know that fear can choke the decision process and cause you to avoid taking risks altogether. Fear also can paralyze you when you need to act quickly and decisively to save yourself or someone else from danger—the deer-in-the-headlights syndrome. All great traders have mastered their fears and are able to act decisively when needed.

Fear disables traders in two ways: It can make them avoid taking risks, and that costs opportunity, and it can make them put their heads in the sand and avoid facing the reality of risks already undertaken by not exiting trades that have turned out poorly. Both these effects of fear can destroy a trader. You must learn to overcome fear to be successful navigating under uncertainty. Some traders must work very hard to overcome their natural tendencies; others find it a bit easier. There are no exceptions: Every great trader has learned how to overcome fear in trading.

Remain Flexible

As a trader, you never know which stock or which market may make a move. This is the essence of uncertainty. You don't know what is going to happen. When you don't know what is going to happen, the best strategy is to be ready for anything.

A trader never knows when a particular market will deliver large returns. She never knows which of the many available markets will make her money. Since they don't know which markets will move, great traders diversify to increase their chances of being successful. This means that they trade in many markets at the same time so that they are able to take advantage of large changes in price movement to make money. The best traders don't care which markets they trade in. They are continuously looking for new markets, and they are continuously looking for new ways of making money while trading.

Traders also know that the trades they put on may end up losing money, so they may need to quickly reverse course. Smart traders also know that there is a limit to how many contracts or shares they can trade without affecting the market. As they exceed this limit, it becomes harder and harder to reverse course. To remain flexible, good traders know that they need to control their position sizes.

[One of the biggest misconceptions is that] open positions with large profits is "risk." Not true, it's volatility. Traders should be more concerned with the risk of losing capital and previously earned/closed profits. Being too concerned with open trade profit by reducing exposure outside the basic exit rules of the [strategy] will result in less capital and real losses.

—**Jerry Parker**,
a fellow Turtle and the CEO of Chesapeake Capital,
a managed futures asset manager with over $1 billion
under management

Take Reasoned Risks

Many beginners trade like they are sitting at a Las Vegas blackjack table. They put too much money at risk, and they trade based on hunches, rumors, or someone else's advice. They take foolish risks. They hope. They pray.

Great traders take reasoned risks. A reasoned risk is more like an educated guess than a roll of the dice. A reasoned risk also limits exposure so that one or a few trades will not affect the trader's account too adversely should the trades turn out badly. Trades with reasoned risks are trades with the following qualities:

- **Reasonable exposure** — enough exposure to make a good return but not so much as to expose the trader to the risk of losing everything in the event of a big adverse price movement.
- **Positive edge** — trading with the odds in your favor.

Great traders only make trades that exhibit both these qualities. Trading too many contracts or with too much leverage is just plain dumb. Trading when the odds are not in your favor is too much like gambling in Vegas. Great traders are not gamblers.

Prepare to Be Wrong

If you don't know what the future will bring and you choose a trade that assumes a particular outcome, it is possible that you will be wrong. And depending on the type of trade, losing money may be the likelier outcome. What matters in the end is the total money won and lost, not whether you were right more often than you were wrong.

Since you probably will make trades that are likely to go wrong, you need to have a plan in place for what you will do in that event, and you need to determine just what things could possibly go wrong. In trading, this means having a price where you will exit a losing trade or a systematic method of dealing with losing trades that eventually will reduce your exposure to the continued risk associated with being wrong to zero.

The familiarity with and embrace of poor outcomes is one of the hallmarks of a great trader. It is also one of the aspects of trading that is most instructive to those who wish to apply the lessons of trading to other areas of human endeavor that involve uncertainty. Many decisions in life have uncertain outcomes. If the outcome is uncertain, then you should have a plan for what to do when the future doesn't have the ideal turnout. This is simple to say but often not so simple to execute.

Actively Seek Reality

As a trader, nothing is more important than an accurate picture of reality. Luckily, finding reality in trading is usually relatively easy. The current price in a given market represents the reality of that market. It doesn't matter what you thought might have happened or what you wish would have happened, the price represents what actually has happened very recently and is happening right now. It represents reality.

In the early 1980s when I first learned about trading, the state-of-the-art trading setup at the time was a satellite feed hooked up to a specialized computer system that would allow traders to see the price of the markets with a delay of perhaps 5 to 10 seconds from the action on the floor. Clerks employed by the exchange sat just outside the floor relaying prices to the exchange's electronic price feeds. These prices, in turn, would be sent via dedicated phone lines to the satellite uploading centers, where they would be relayed to customers throughout the world. Most successful traders spent—and still spend—somewhere between \$300 and \$500 per month to receive up-to-date quotations of the current prices. This was money well spent.

Traders know that their decisions will result in losses. They also realize that they need to be aware as soon as possible when these losses happen. A focus on what the market actually does, the market's reality, keeps successful traders from burying their heads in the sand and pretending that the world is other than it actually is.

Respond Quickly to Change

Just as important as actively seeking and facing reality is your response when that reality turns out to be not what you had hoped for. When the market moves to price levels where a trader had previously determined he would get out of a trade, a competent trader will respond quickly and get out, thereby reducing his exposure to continued uncertainty to zero.

To do otherwise is just plain dumb. In trading, this seems obvious, yet for many traders—especially new ones—this act can be gut-wrenching and soul-withering. The problem is often the attachment to one's previous opinion. To change quickly, you must become very comfortable with the idea of being wrong. It must become easy. Attaining the required level of comfort is often very difficult, and many traders succumb to a paralysis of hesitation and inaction that sometimes causes them to lose their entire account. In some cases, this paralysis has resulted in losses that have bankrupted an entire firm, for example, Brian Hunter at Amaranth Advisors (\$6 billion) and Nick Leeson at Barings Bank (\$1.4 billion).

Focus on Decisions, Not Outcomes

One of the reasons that great traders can so easily change course is that they have a sophisticated and accurate view of the meaning of error concerning decisions made under uncertainty. They understand that the fact that things did not turn out the way they had hoped does not necessarily mean that taking the trade was a mistake. They know that many times good ideas don't work out. The very presence of uncertainty ensures that some trades will be wrong part of the time.

In contrast, most losing traders don't have a strategy for their trades. They don't have a plan at all. They shoot from the hip. Use their gut. Or it might be more accurate perhaps to say that they guess. This is so because many novices don't understand uncertainty or how to make money from trading.

Great traders have a strategy. They have analyzed the markets they trade, and they have tested their strategies to make certain that they work. This research also has taught them how they will know when they are right or wrong. They know when to buy and when to sell. Some great traders have their rules and strategy detailed so specifically that they can have a computer tell them when to buy and sell. Other great traders have their strategy outlined in broader terms that they apply in real time using their brains to fill in the details. All great traders put trades on for a particular reason, and they take them off for a particular reason. No great trader guesses.

The do-or-die nature of trading with its global competition, rapid decisions, and huge monetary potential offers a raw glimpse into the power and danger of decision making under uncertainty. The crucible of trading is a good basis for understanding the importance of facing and overcoming fear as well as taking only reasoned risk. In later chapters I will draw on more specifics from trading to show how overcoming fear is an important rule in other areas where you need to make decisions under uncertainty.

Entrepreneurs—by comparison—operate in a slower, more deliberate, and planned environment, which makes it easier to understand how important it is to be flexible, to know when you are wrong, and to actively seek reality. Whereas the lessons from emergency room doctors make it easier to understand how important it is to respond quickly to change and to focus on decisions, not outcomes. By examining risk and uncertainty from these three different perspectives, you can get a more complete sense of the seven rules for risk.

In Chapter 5 I will explain how the seven rules apply to starting and running businesses.

UNCERTAIN BUSINESS

A lot of what goes into starting companies is turning nothing into something. Starting with a blank slate, and just inventing all kinds of stuff. . . . You'll never know if it's ultimately correct. You just have to use your judgment, make decisions, and move on. . . . To some people, that's pretty scary. Not to have any answers to look up in the back of the book.

—Stephen Wolfram

I have been interested in business since 1980. In that year, I was 16 years old and went to work after school for George Arndt, an entrepreneur in the town where I lived. It was a small software company that sold programs for commodity traders and those who aspired to be one.

I worked in an office that was in the owner's home. It was a small New England house with two bedrooms and a lot of animals. We had to run a gauntlet of geese and one crazed turkey each day to get in and out of the house. I quickly learned that geese, and especially the turkey, could smell fear. If you ran at them, they would scatter; if you walked timidly, they would peck at your legs as you passed by. The turkey was the most aggressive and the largest of the lot.

Our desks consisted of the kitchen table and one folding table off to the side of the kitchen. It was chaotic and disorganized but much more interesting than high school.

What really appealed to me was the freedom of programming. I was given certain tasks, and I was responsible for deciding how to do the work. It was the first time I had ever used a computer. I still smile to think that I got my first job programming before actually having learned to program. To this day, I don't think George knows this.

Earlier in the year, I had seen my first computer program running on the computer on display at the Radio Shack store in Ayer, Massachusetts, about three miles from where I lived. A local engineer from DEC (Digital Equipment Corporation)—one of the world's largest computer companies at the time, which was headquartered in Maynard, Massachusetts, about 10 miles away—had written a program that scrolled his name diagonally across the screen. He showed me the three lines of code, and I was hooked.

I bought the advanced Basic language reference manual because although my family could not afford the $1,000+ for a computer, I wanted to learn how to program it and see how it worked. I read the manual a couple of times, and it seemed relatively simple. You typed in commands that told the computer what to do, then you typed "run," and the computer ran the code on each of the lines one at a time. Simple enough.

From time to time, I stopped by the Radio Shack in Ayer and typed in a few lines.

Then, in the fall of 1980, my sister Valerie answered an ad in the local paper for a bookkeeping position for George Arndt at his small software company. George also was hiring local high school students to do some programming after school. My sister told me to apply. I knew some of the kids that got jobs, and I figured I was smarter than they were, so I went with my sister one day to see if I could get a job. George told me that the positions had already been filled. I was mildly discouraged. However, since I had a combined total of about two hours' programming experience, I hadn't thought I would land the job anyway.

About four or five weeks later, my sister said that George was interested in having me come in. George was very disappointed in the work of most of the other students, and my sister had been talking me up. So I came in one Friday after school to see him.

The interview was very short. He said: "I'll give you a job for the next week. If you can do the work, I will keep you on as an employee. If not, it will be your last week." So I had a job as a programmer. If I could program, I would keep the job. This was a low-risk hire for George and a great opportunity for me.

The problem was, I didn't really know how to program. So I spent the weekend reading the *TRS-80 Level II Basic Reference Manual* over and over again, hoping that cramming would substitute for experience.

It worked. I kept that job for the next three years, during my last year in high school and while I attended college before dropping out to trade commodities. That job introduced me to trading and to my first trading mentor, Rotchy Barker, and ultimately provided me with the background to be one of the 12 people selected for the training program run by the famous trader Richard Dennis that became known as the *Turtle Program*.

The way I obtained my first job in programming is a good example of a trait of successful entrepreneurs: They are comfortable taking risks. They jump right in without knowing exactly what lies ahead. They are willing to potentially waste their time trying something that may not work out.

In the rest of this chapter we will look at the seven rules for mastering risk in greater detail from the point of view of business entrepreneurs and the people who invest in startups, angel investors, and venture capitalists. In the startup environment, three of the rules stand out as particularly important: organizing for flexibility, preparing to be wrong, and actively seeking reality.

The reason that these three rules are so important is that the type of uncertainty that exists in a startup is different from the type of uncertainty that exists in trading. In a startup, the uncertainty is generally informational uncertainty—which comes because entrepreneurs must act within a limited timeframe, and they generally have insufficient resources to explore all potential choices to the degree required to eliminate uncertainty. So entrepreneurs have to make educated guesses.

In the process of starting the business and proceeding according to plans that reflect all the educated guesses taken in aggregate, an entrepreneur comes to find out that some, perhaps many, or even most of those guesses were wrong. Some will be wrong in minor ways: Some expenses may be slightly lower than expected, revenues may fluctuate more than expected, it may take longer than expected to get all the permits required to open the business, and other minor things. Some of the guesses will be completely wrong, perhaps catastrophically so.

When this happens, an entrepreneur who has organized for flexibility, who has prepared to be wrong, and who has been actively seeking reality will not be easily shaken. She will adapt her new venture as reality unfolds to seek success in that new reality. A great entrepreneur knows that being wrong is not a problem; the problem is never expecting to be wrong and *staying wrong* when reality comes knocking.

Consider the seven rules for mastering risk again from the point of view of an entrepreneur:

1. Overcome fear.
2. Remain flexible.
3. Take reasoned risks.
4. Prepare to be wrong.
5. Actively seek reality.
6. Respond quickly to change.
7. Focus on decisions, not outcomes.

Overcome Fear

Many people dream of running their own business. Perhaps they get tired of working where they don't have much say in the work they do. Perhaps they disagree with their boss or management on certain ethical issues. Perhaps they have an idea they think will make a difference in the world. For most people, this dream will stay a dream. It will not make the transition from dream to plan to reality.

Others go one step further. They plan for the day when they will start their own business. They talk to all their friends about their idea. They build sales projections and marketing plans and budgets and dream of all the money they will make and the freedom their new business will bring. And they save up money and wait for the perfect environment for starting their new business. But they never seem to actually take the concrete step of quitting their job to make a go in the new business.

Make no mistake about it. Starting a business is scary. It is risky. You could lose everything. Most people simply do not have the appetite for risk that is required to be successful in a startup.

If you want to be successful as an entrepreneur, you must learn to be comfortable with taking risks under uncertain conditions. You must be willing to risk everything and lose if you want to win.

Remain Flexible

When you don't know what the future will bring, then you need to be prepared to be wrong. You need to be organized to be wrong. This is what flexibility means. Since you know you can't predict the future with complete accuracy, it only makes sense to organize your business in a way that can compensate for the mistakes in prediction, for the bad guesses that are part of any venture.

Remaining flexible in a startup includes four important ideas:

1. **A flexible team.** A small group of smart people who are able and willing to do three or four jobs at the same time instead of a larger group of people who only know how to do one thing. The team should be composed of people with broad experience as much as possible rather than deep experience in one specific area. The key to remaining flexible is to have a team of people who are psychologically well suited to a startup environment. Some people just plain aren't ready for a startup.

2. **A flexible plan.** The plan must be flexible and account for several different outcomes. There should be plans that account for very conservative estimates or revenues, expected revenues, and worst-case revenues; that is, what do you do if there are no sales at all?

3. **Alternative revenue streams.** If possible, the plan should include alternate products or services that can be provided by the startup team. If revenues for the main product do not pan out or take longer than expected, alternate revenue streams can keep the company alive.

4. **A strategic reserve.** Some money and other resources should be kept in reserve. Having a reserve will allow you to compensate for the likely divergence between the original plan and the reality you find as the business develops.

Take Reasoned Risks

In startups, the investment risk involved is generally well known ahead of time. You can *lose all the money you have personally invested* if the new company cannot get to the point where it makes money or has created enough value in its products and assets to warrant a sale to another company.

Not all risks are investment risks. In fact, the most important risks in a startup have nothing to do with the investment losses. There are

Market risks. Are you entering a market with a large competitor? Are you entering a market that requires large up-front capital costs?

Capital risks. Will you need ongoing infusions of capital to grow the business to profitability? Will you be able to secure that capital in the event that the capital market environment changes?

Personnel risks. How many members of the startup team have already done the job they need to do? How many of them are learning new jobs? How many of them can fill in to help mentor others or replace them temporarily if required?

Technology risks. Are you using new, untried technologies? Are there less risky alternatives? Is your team expert in these new technologies or sufficiently experienced to manage them effectively?

In general, it makes sense to reduce the number of areas where you are taking risks to as few as possible. Use proven technologies if you can. If you need to use new technology, make sure that you have an experienced technology team. Use proven team members if you can. Raise all the money you need before starting if you can. Or even better, come up with a plan that requires little or no money. A plan that has an experienced and flexible team on which everyone is capable of doing many of the other team members' jobs, that uses technology they already understand, and that has sufficient capital at the outset to complete the plan will have a much better chance of success.

In order to be an entrepreneur, you need to have a slightly defective perception of risk. Starting a company is extremely difficult and you face many ups and downs along the way. Normal people become discouraged and give up. One key to being a successful entrepreneur is being able to ignore the volatility and remain optimistic.

But this trait is a double-edged sword.

Many entrepreneurs have risk calculators stuck in the optimistic position; that is why so many vacillate continuously from boom to bust. A willingness to accept risk makes one successful, but it can also lead to eventual ruin.

In many cases, the role of the venture capitalist is to help temper this manic cycle. Part of the value creation process is harnessing the power of optimism in the early days, while helping the entrepreneur to avoid falling victim to its continued seduction once a later stage has been reached.

—Simon Olson,
partner at the venture capital firm
DFJ FIR Capital

Prepare to Be Wrong

The first step in preparing to be wrong is to acknowledge that the future will not bring what you think it will. So you need to decide ahead of time what events or lack thereof, what measures, what confluence of events will indicate that a particular "guess" about the future embodied in your plans was wrong and what you will do about it in that event.

Preparing to be wrong means having clear measurements and a clear strategy for what to do when things don't turn out as you hope. In some cases, it may even mean shutting down the business in an orderly manner.

The important thing is to have thought through ahead of time how you will know if things are going according to plan or not. If you do this thinking ahead of time, you may discover ways to save the business if your original plan was off base by a large margin. If you wait until reality diverges from your plan, you may be so busy trying to save a sinking ship that you don't have the time or the energy to reverse course.

Actively Seek Reality

This is perhaps the rule that most commonly distinguishes the successful from the failed startup teams. Winning teams are always looking out for indications of errors. Losing teams are always trying to pretend that they are right when reality is demonstrating otherwise. Losing teams spend too much time trying to justify their previous decisions and too little time changing course.

Sometimes reality is not so easy to find. An inspirational CEO may find that her team hides the truth because they don't want to disappoint her. A harsh CEO may find that his team hides the truth out of fear of retribution. Even in a small team of 20 to 30 people it can be difficult to keep tabs on all parts of the company down to the level of detail necessary to ensure success in a risky venture. Reality may be hard to find.

So successful entrepreneurs expend a lot of time, money, and effort making sure that things are going according to plan. The reason that this is so important is that minor deviations from forecast reality, if caught early enough, may only require minor adjustments to the plan. If these same problems are not caught early, they may doom the entire venture.

This can be a bit like driving a car. New drivers have a hard time processing all the new information. They often focus so much on the mechanics of driving that they fail to notice a red light. They may then stop suddenly as they see the light very late and have to slam on the brakes to avoid an accident. An experienced driver will be looking for a light change the entire time that she is approaching an intersection. If it changes, there will be a smooth stop.

A safe defensive driver also will be watching other traffic closely to make sure that the traffic is actually stopped or in the process of stopping before the safe driver enters the intersection. A safe driver doesn't assume that other cars are all paying attention because he knows from experience that it only takes one driver not paying attention to cause an accident.

Smart CEOs do the same thing. They watch their own job, but they also keep watch over the entire team and company just in case someone else is not paying enough attention. If caught early, mistakes and inattention generally will not be fatal. If caught late, you may have a crash on your hands. I know. I've crashed hard more than once. I had to learn this rule the hard way.

Respond Quickly to Change

As important as it is to be paying attention and actively seeking reality, it is also very important to react quickly to changes in the environment that indicate that a plan needs adjustment. Speed is important.

If early indications are that potential customers do not like the product, the time to react is at that point, not 10 days later, not 2 months later, not after the product ships and sales are dismal. Find out what they don't like and why—and fix it—as soon as you see indications of a problem.

Early course corrections are relatively painless and easy to effect. Late course corrections may not even be possible. Consider a super-tanker heading into port. One hundred miles out, it may take only a tiny, imperceptible change in heading to avoid a large obstacle. One mile out, it might take a heroic effort with one engine reversed and the wheel all the way to starboard. At 100 yards away, there may be no way to avoid the obstacle; the physics just won't allow it. This is one reason that sailors try to stay well clear of supertankers; if you get in their way it is probable that they can't avoid hitting you, and you will get crushed.

Focus on Decisions, Not Outcomes

One of the reasons that a good team is not afraid to change course is because they have a mature understanding of uncertainty. They know that they will be wrong. So they have no problem reversing course or changing plans when indications warrant. They know that what matters is how well you make decisions with the information you have at the time, not how often you are right or wrong.

They also know that being wrong early and changing course early are often the quickest way to find the correct course. They know that you often don't have enough information to know the correct course until you try an incorrect one. Then, through the process of trying an incorrect approach, it becomes obvious what should have been done. At these times, making reasoned decisions with continuously updated information is the best way to find a workable approach.

Great teams don't expect to be able to predict the future with 100 percent accuracy. They don't expect that all their plans will be perfect. They are comfortable with a fuzzy sense of what the future will bring, knowing that with their flexible plan, flexible team, and constant monitoring, they will be able to be successful even if that future brings something they did not at all expect from the start. For entrepreneurs, flexibility and responsiveness are paramount.

In Chapter 6 I will examine the ways that emergency room doctors use the seven rules for mastering risk.

THE RISK DOCTORS

How very little can be done under a spirit of fear.
—Florence Nightingale

In the summer of 2000, I lived a few blocks from the main street, University Avenue, in Palo Alto, California. This was the very heart of Silicon Valley. Stanford University was about a mile up the road. Perhaps half the venture capitalists in Silicon Valley had their main offices within a couple of miles from where I lived.

Sun Microsystems, Hewlett-Packard, Google—they all had started there. Palo Alto also was the location for the famous Xerox PARC (Palo Alto Research Center) that had invented Ethernet networking, used for most of the Internet, the mouse, as well as the graphical interface later marketed by Apple in the Macintosh and by Microsoft with Windows, among many other widely used inventions.

One of the amazing things about Silicon Valley was the concentration of really bright people with a similar outlook on life. In Palo Alto, especially at the height of the Internet bubble in 1998 through 2000, everyone was involved in startups and very optimistic about the future. If you went out anywhere, you would constantly run into people working in small groups with others as members of a new startup company.

One beautiful Saturday I happened to be sitting in the small park that was located equidistant from home and work reading a recent book by Larry Downes. While I was reading, a guy in his late 20s who had been reading another book a few benches down walked by and asked me if I liked the book I was reading. He told me that he knew Larry, who had been a professor of his while he had attended Northwestern Law School a few years earlier. We chatted for a bit, and then I continued reading. Over the next few months, I continued to see the same guy in the park near my home, and we continued to talk about start-ups, strategy, and business. His name was Simon Olson, and he became my good friend.

Toward the end of the year, Simon started telling me that he was going to work with a friend of his from Northwestern, Bruce Tizes. Bruce was forming a new hedge fund in the Virgin Islands. At first, I had no idea what a hedge fund was because I had not spent any time in finance or trading for about 15 years. After a while, though, I started to infer that hedge funds had something to do with trading. So I asked Simon if he had ever heard of the Turtles. He said that of course he had. While I was a bit surprised, I told him that I had been one the Turtles.

He subsequently told his friend Bruce about me, and the next time that Bruce was in the area, we had lunch. Bruce and I chatted about the possibility of my coming to the Virgin Islands to join the new hedge fund they were forming. These discussions took place at the point in time when it was obvious to most people that the Internet party was over in Silicon Valley and pink slips were flying everywhere. So I thought it might be a good time to do something new for a few years. I had often thought about getting back into trading, so I entertained Bruce's potential offer with interest. After a few months of discussion, I decided to join Bruce and Simon in their hedge fund venture, and Bruce and I subsequently became good friends.

The Doctor, the Lawyer, and the Trader

Bruce had a very interesting background. He was incredibly bright, with a very flexible mind. He had graduated high school at 15 years of age, college at 16, and medical school at 20. He later made a lot of money investing in real estate and trading stocks. While in his late 30s, Bruce earned a law degree at Northwestern University in Chicago, where he had met Simon.

For most of the time since he had become a doctor, Bruce had been practicing emergency medicine at Mount Sinai Hospital in Chicago. Mount Sinai is the inspiration for the television series *ER* that also takes place in Chicago. It is a major destination for accident and gunshot victims in the downtown Chicago area.

In various discussions over lunch or dinner over the few years we worked together, I came to learn a bit about the life of an emergency room doctor. At one point I told Bruce how in my personal experience doctors did not make very good traders. He agreed in general but told me that he thought that ER doctors were an exception. Over time, he convinced me, and I came to see there were similarities in how ER doctors and traders approached risk and uncertainty.

Most of you are familiar with many of the aspects of life-or-death emergencies, having experienced them when you or a loved one has been seriously sick or injured. So it may be a little easier to understand uncertainty if you examine it from the perspective of an ER doctor. In the next few sections I will take a look at the seven rules for mastering risk from the perspective of an ER doctor. Once again, the seven rules are

1. Overcome fear.

2. Remain flexible.

3. Take reasoned risks.

4. Prepare to be wrong.

5. Actively seek reality.

6. Respond quickly to change

7. Focus on decisions, not outcomes.

Overcome Fear

Risk is everywhere in the ER. You can't avoid it. Do nothing, and the patient may die. Do the wrong thing, and the patient may die. Do the right thing, and the patient still may die. You can't avoid risk.

At times, there may be so many patients requiring assistance that it becomes impossible to give them all care. Yet decisions must be made. The time element is critical to emergency care, and this greatly increases the risk associated with delay or making the wrong decisions. The doctor must make decisions quickly when the ER is busy, and these decisions are extremely important. Unlike in trading or in a startup, in the ER, mistakes can kill someone.

To be successful as an ER doctor, you must be able to handle life-or-death decisions every day. You must have the confidence in your own abilities and your own judgment to act quickly when there is very little time. No doctor who is afraid to make life-or-death decisions stays in ER for very long.

In every emergency requiring a life saving or life sustaining procedure, there is a sense of fear and apprehension, especially if the patient's condition suddenly deteriorates. The other day I had a patient come into the ER with minor chest discomfort. She was talking without difficulty and we joked around a bit, she said her discomfort was present for a couple of days (didn't seem too emer-

gent). I ordered routine tests to rule out some of the worse case scenarios (but didn't expect to find much). Suddenly, she became short of breath and her vitals were deteriorating. I needed to act fast. My training and experience kept me calm in the eyes of the patient and the staff, but internally I felt great fear and knew I had to overcome it. I placed a large needle and catheter (chest tube) into her anterior chest and it expressed a large hiss of air. Luckily, her condition quickly improved. In this case, my actions resolved the problem. She had a collapsed lung that was trapping air in her chest and it was pushing on her heart, blood vessels and her other lung. If I was unsuccessful she could have died.

I had to overcome the fear first in order to make the move and begin the procedure. Fear makes you second guess yourself. What if the procedure failed and she continued to deteriorate? What else could be wrong and what if I couldn't find it in time? We can't control the outcomes of illnesses with absolute certainty. We can, however, predict outcomes with a degree of certainty, based on experience, training, and case studies, but there will always be a degree of uncertainty. In trading, we can use backtesting, technical analysis and experience to support our decisions on what to trade and when to enter a trade. Still, the outcome of the trade will always be uncertain and therefore will always create a degree of fear. It is this fear that must be overcome in order to make the right trade at the right time.

—Ted Patras M.D.,
physician, board member and manager partner at EHP Corp., a multi-hospital Chicago-area practice management group in emergency medicine. (Dr. Patras has also been trading options and futures for 15 years.)

Remain Flexible

One of the hallmarks of an ER facility is the ability to act very quickly to address virtually any type of critical medical need. A well-equipped ER will have diagnostic and surgical facilities onsite, defibrillators for heart attack victims, and even surgical tools for those times when a patient may not survive the trip up the elevator to a full surgical suite.

Another way that an ER facility organizes for flexibility is by making sure that there are sufficient doctors with a broad range of specialties available. ERs don't staff for the average workload; they staff for the maximum expected workload. They keep a strategic reserve of doctors and nurses available to assist in case things get extremely busy.

Take Reasoned Risks

Triage is one way of managing the risks associated with the uncertainty of medical diagnoses and treatments. Triage is a way of sorting patients so those who require immediate assistance are helped first, those in potentially critical situations next, and those in no imminent danger of further damage are helped last. For example, if you go to the ER with a broken leg, you may or may not be the first person in line for treatment. If a shooting victim comes in, you will be shuffled back in line. Your injury, while serious, can wait because you are in little danger of dying, and a few hours' delay in setting a bone is unlikely to cause permanent damage.

Diagnosis itself is one of the most important aspects of emergency treatment. The wrong diagnosis can kill a patient. The right diagnosis can save a life. Yet diagnosis is messy. There are no right answers, only probable answers.

Doctors weigh the probability of particular diseases or injuries against the seriousness of outcomes for the likely conditions and the time sensitivity of a given treatment. Some problems require immediate care, whereas some are less urgent. Good doctors can quickly evaluate the symptoms and results of diagnostic tests to deliver the best diagnosis. The diagnosis may be wrong, but a good doctor will evaluate the factors to determine the most likely one and will continue to run tests to eliminate rarer but potentially more serious problems in time to effect relevant treatment.

When you put on a trade, you don't know what the outcome is going to be. In acute medicine, don't know what the outcome will be. So you can't try to predict or force a particular outcome. You need to be thinking on your feet and always ready to adjust to the new data as they arrive.

—Ted Patras, M.D.

Prepare to Be Wrong

A preliminary diagnosis may be wrong; the onset of more serious symptoms may indicate that a problem is more urgent than anticipated initially. Doctors know this. This is why they and their staff continuously monitor the health status of their patients.

Often while the initial diagnosis is being treated doctors will order additional tests to verify the correctness of that initial diagnosis. They know they can be wrong in their assessment. So they allow for this by checking for alternatives even while treating for the current diagnosis.

More than perhaps any other experts in uncertainty, doctors understand the ways that uncertainty can manifest itself. As a profession, doctors have almost completely mapped the current thinking in medicine into a large tree of objective and even subjective tests that can be run to confirm or eliminate a particular diagnosis. So a doctor knows exactly how to tell if she is wrong and what to do in that event almost every time she makes a diagnosis. Doctors also know which other less common medical problems also can exhibit the same symptoms that the previous diagnosis did.

For example, if a patient comes in with a medium-grade fever, a doctor normally will check the ears, nose, sinuses, lymph nodes, and breathing to eliminate organ-specific issues and then probably issue a diagnosis of a flu infection. If the fever rises above 102 degrees, the doctor probably will start running some tests to eliminate more serious problems, such as a bacterial infection or viral meningitis.

It is so difficult for most people to admit being wrong. Trading, and emergency medicine, both frequently use inductive reasoning (starting at the end and working backwards from that result). Overtly acknowledging the possibility of being wrong allows prospective planning to optimize results. It also, impliedly, allows for the possibility of being correct, which also allows prospective planning.

—Bruce Tizes, M.D. J.D.,
managing director at Galt Capital and former emergency room physician at Mount Sinai Hospital in Chicago which was the inspiration for the television series *ER*

Actively Seek Reality

Since doctors are not 100 percent certain that the diagnosis they have made for a given patient is correct, they continue to monitor that patient's health. If the patient is in serious danger, he will be monitored continuously. Anyone who visits a hospital emergency room will notice all the various monitors and diagnostic machines. There are ECG monitors to check the general health of the heart, pulse monitors, blood oxygenation testers, etc. The ER staff always has up-to-the-second status for their patients. These immediate readings alert doctors and nurses quickly to changes indicating a worsening condition.

Once the monitors have been set up (generally by the nursing staff), ER doctors double-check their diagnosis by running tests to rule out more serious illnesses or injuries that may be less common. The more serious the patient's condition, the more tests will be run. A small error in diagnosis may cost a patient's life if she suffers from a serious condition with poor vital signs such as very low blood pressure or an erratic pulse. A large error in diagnosis may not matter for a patient who is relatively healthy. So more time and effort are spent to verify the diagnoses of patients with more serious conditions, and less time and effort are spent verifying the diagnoses of stable patients.

Actively seeking reality is extremely important in emergency medicine because initial diagnoses are likely to be in error to some degree a significant percentage of the time. Since misdiagnoses can kill people, much time and effort are spent to verify and check a diagnosis and to make sure that a patient does not regress.

Respond Quickly to Change

If caught early, a misdiagnosis or a significant change in a patient's condition need not be cause for worry. If caught late, it can mean serious complications, extended hospitalization, or even death. For critical illness and injury, time is very important.

The entire point of closely monitoring a patient is to enable the doctor to quickly determine if there is something more serious wrong than was first evident. A doctor's initial diagnosis comes from the symptoms that are readily apparent. A good doctor knows that there may be a more serious condition causing those symptoms. More serious conditions often warrant different treatment. Sometimes a patient's condition is serious enough that a few hours can mean the difference between life and death or between full recovery and permanent brain damage.

For example, a mother comes into the ER with her preteen son, who is running a fever of 102 degrees, has a headache, and is vomiting. These are most likely symptoms from a flu infection that is not particularly emergent. The treatment for the flu is normally just bed rest and drinking lots of fluids. So, if the ER is busy, the flu patient normally will wait as patients with more urgent problems get care.

The addition of one more symptom may change the treatment completely. If the patient who may have been sitting in the ER waiting room starts complaining of a stiff painful neck in addition to the flu symptoms, this may be indicative of spinal meningitis, which is a life-threatening disease if not treated quickly. The attending physician likely will order an immediate lumbar puncture (also called a *spinal tap*) to examine the spinal fluid to see if it is infected with the organisms that cause spinal meningitis. If it is a bacterial infection, treatment with antibiotics will begin right away. A few hours difference can save a life in the case of bacterial spinal meningitis.

The important thing to remember is that a good doctor knows what to look for that will indicate a more serious condition than was indicated initially. She also will respond very quickly to administer appropriate treatment when the symptoms or tests indicate a more serious condition. A good doctor is not afraid of being wrong. A good doctor is looking for any sign that she might have been wrong so that she can help the patient who has a more serious disease in time to treat it so the patient can recover completely.

Focus on Decisions, Not Outcomes

One of the difficulties facing ER doctors because of the uncertainty of medical diagnoses and treatments is the fact that a doctor can do everything correctly, and the patient still may die or suffer permanent damage. The doctor might perform perfectly and still lose the patient.

"Focus on decisions, not outcomes" is an essential viewpoint shift from what is uncontrollable to what can be controlled by discipline and rigorous prior thought. All of the other rules are implicit in this rule.

—Bruce Tizes

At times, a patient may require risky surgery to save his life. The doctor will weigh the risk of the surgery itself against the risk of alternative treatments. If the surgery will increase the chances of the patient surviving, then the doctor will order the surgery or perform it herself in cases of extreme emergency.

A doctor may make the best decision under the circumstances using the very best information available, and still the patient may die. A good doctor will evaluate the decision not on the basis of how it turns out but according to the relative probabilities of the outcomes themselves. An outcome of a dead patient does not mean that surgery was a mistake. Likewise, it may be that the surgery should not have been performed even when it has a successful outcome.

If ER doctors evaluated their decisions on the basis of outcomes, then it would lead to bad medicine. For example, if a particular surgery has a 10 percent mortality rate, meaning that 10 percent of the patients who have the surgery die soon after, this is risky surgery. If a patient has an injury that will kill the patient 60 percent of the time without that surgery, then the correct action is to have the surgery performed because the patient will be six times more likely to live with it than without it. If an ER doctor orders the surgery and it is performed without error, the patient still may die. This does not change the fact that absent any new information, the decision to have the surgery still was correct.

> *When bad things occur we often second-guess ourselves. Bad things happen despite what we do.*
>
> —Ted Patras, M.D.

The inherent uncertainty of diagnosis and treatment means that many times the right treatment will have a bad outcome. A good doctor knows this and will continue prescribing the best possible treatment even when a few rare examples of bad outcome cross her path.

In the next seven chapters I will discuss the seven rules for mastering risk in greater detail. In these examples I will draw on the sophisticated understanding of traders, entrepreneurs, and ER doctors to illustrate the seven rules. As you read these chapters, you will notice how the approach taken by these three groups reflects a common perspective on uncertainty and risk.

FEAR—THE MIND KILLER

I must not fear.
Fear is the mind-killer.
Fear is the little-death that brings total obliteration.
I will face my fear.
I will permit it to pass over me and through me.
—Frank Herbert, "Litany Against Fear" from *Dune*

I had been waiting almost a month for this flight. On three separate Saturdays, my friend Tyson Langdon and I had driven the hour to the airport only to be told that we could not fly. The winds were too high—too high for beginners anyway.

Finally, at the end of yet another long Saturday spent waiting for the winds to die down, the instructors told us that only one of us could fly. Tyson said that he wasn't feeling it, so I could fly. Our plane was a Cessna 206, a small six-seat plane with an overhead wing and fixed landing gear, the vehicle of our aspirations. I wanted to jump out of it. From the time I was in my early teens, I had an informal list of the crazy things I wanted to do in my life. Some of them I had checked off years earlier. On that winter day in 2001, I was going to check off skydiving.

My friend Alan had been telling me about the skydiving drop zone where he camped out for three days every weekend. Alan was a skydiving instructor and had made about 9,000 separate jumps. I used to meet him and his skydiving buddies on Wednesday nights at the Gordon Biersch microbrewery two blocks from my home in Palo Alto. For over a year, I had been hearing stories of skydiving exploits. I was about to join them.

Skydiving had seemed like a lot of fun. While waiting for the weather to clear, Tyson and I had watched many skydiving videos. The most interesting were the ones of people floating around in the air doing what looked like a three-dimensional dance in what I later learned is a form of skydiving called *free flying*. Some of them even did this while upside down. It looked like they were actually flying their own bodies. I wanted to try that. Be like one of the birds, even if only a very heavy one with very small wings. I had had plenty of time to think of flying around in the sky like a bird by the time we got the go-ahead to actually jump.

I suited up in one of the student jump suits and put on my harness. I didn't have my own parachute because I was going to jump tandem, which all my skydiving friends recommended for my first jump. Essentially, I was a passenger. Two of us would be attached to the same parachute, with my instructor, a woman about 6 inches shorter and 70 pounds lighter than me, doing the flying.

Since I weighed a bit over 200 pounds, she was going to have her work cut out for her. In order to safely open the parachute, we both needed to be in a stable nonspinning fall. Otherwise, if we were spinning, we might end up entangling in the parachute lines. So I was instructed to put my hands and arms far out and to arch my back. This would allow the instructor to compensate for any poor form on my part and keep us both safe.

Since I had spent almost a thousand hours in small planes as a pilot or copilot and had learned to fly in the 206's little brother, the Cessna 172, I was very comfortable with the takeoff and climb to altitude. I was feeling good and excited to jump. As we got close to our jump altitude of 10,500 feet, my instructor approached and locked our two harnesses together. I was now bound tightly to my instructor with strong nylon webbing and large stainless steel hooks.

I think it was the sound of the wind at 120 mph as the door opened that caused my fear to surface. I was warned about this, but the warning did little good. I was scared. This was not just a normal small plane flight like the hundreds I had taken before. This time I would be jumping out.

My job—a relatively easy one, it seemed to me while I was on the ground—was to place my foot on the small aluminum step by the wheel. This would allow me to make sure that we didn't get tangled with the wheel while exiting. I soon found out that sticking your foot and leg into a 120 mph windstream is not as simple as it looks. The wind was blowing my foot and leg with enough force that I had to use a lot of leg muscle, and it was hard to place my foot exactly where I wanted.

The other problem was that I am very afraid of heights. I remember as a kid having to sit out when my older brother and younger sister climbed the large slide at the county fair because I became too afraid going up the stairs. Even now, I really hate climbing observation towers because they usually have very open stairs. I get a strong sense of visceral fear whenever I look over the edge of a cliff or a high balcony. So looking out over the ground through that open door triggered my primal fear impulse. But I was determined to go anyway.

My instructor—who probably had seen her fair share of frightened first-timers—was trying to help by pushing me out the door. I felt a strong shove, and we tumbled end over end into the blast of air. In a few seconds we were free and stable. I spent the next 60 seconds watching the ground come closer, all the while thinking that skydiving was a complete mind blower. Never before had I had watched the ground with such a sense of the power of gravity. The noise overwhelmed my ears, and the wind felt so strong that it seemed as if we floated on the air as we descended.

Now, if this was all there was to my story, it wouldn't have much purpose here in this book about risk and this chapter about fear. What's the big deal? So I was afraid jumping out of a plane. Most people would consider that a fairly rational response, nothing to be worried about. Except that it didn't end there. That brief 60-second fall stirred something in me. I wanted to fly again by myself. I was hooked. But there was just this problem of actually having to leave the airplane. I really dreaded the prospect of doing that again.

Facing Fear

I figured if I was going to do it, I might as well jump right in. I signed up for the eight jumps required to get my skydiving license, paying cash up front. I also got another friend of mine to sign up with me. We had to come in early Saturday morning for the full-day class for what was known as *level one*—skydiving with training wheels. I physically left the plane with my own parachute and two instructors who followed me down until I opened my chute to make sure I figured out how to get into a stable falling position and got the parachute open successfully. After that, it was my job to steer the parachute to the landing zone and land without hitting anyone or anything on the ground, such as buildings, telephone lines, and such.

The jump plane for that second jump, my first solo jump, was a much larger plane, a de Havilland Twin Otter. It has two large turbo-prop engines under a large overhead wing. The normal four-foot by five-foot aluminum cargo door in the jump plane had been replaced with a door that rolled into the plane like the cover for a roll-top desk. This type of door could be opened and closed while the plane was flying. There was also a stainless steel bar about six inches above the door on the outside. The bar was a handhold so that many skydivers could exit the plane at the same time. This bar was handy for formation flying because as many as eight skydivers could jump from the plane at once.

I was instructed to climb out and stand up outside the plane and wait for the two instructors to appear beside me. We couldn't hear in the roar of the wind at 120 mph, so I was instructed to look at each one and nod so that they knew I was okay. Then we were to bend down together using our knee bending to communicate our timing in a count of one, two, and let go together on three.

Stepping out of the plane, I noticed the windstream was much stronger than I encountered outside the Cessna 206 on my first jump. The Twin Otter's left engine was directly in front of the door, so in addition to the normal airflow caused by the plane's movement, there was a strong blast from the engine's propeller. This increased my anxiety again. I was not terrified in the sense of feeling some intense foreboding danger, but I was anxious from too many new sensory inputs with no prior experience to put them into context.

Too much of this new sensory experience made it important for me to be calm, cool, and collected. This wasn't some amusement park ride. My life depended on my ability to perform at a basic level.

As we left the plane and started descending, my anxiety lessened. I pulled my ripcord, flew the now open chute as a glider, and landed in the drop zone. Most modern parachutes are ram-air parafoils that are wing-shaped. They fly much like a paraglider. As a private pilot, I felt pretty comfortable with flying the parachute because it was similar in many respects to flying and landing a small plane.

Over the course of the next month or so, I made the eight jumps required for certification as a skydiver under the U.S. Parachuting Association. With each successive jump, my anxiety with leaving the plane dropped noticeably.

The seventh jump was an exception. Instead of climbing slowly to exit the plane, one of the challenges for this jump was to exit the plane by jumping headfirst with my arms extended into the air as one might jump into a swimming pool. Since I hated leaving the plane, and I had been told about the entire curriculum from my first jump, I let my dread for the seventh jump build up.

As we climbed into the plane, I decided that the only way to get through the jump would be to just go for it. When my turn came, I placed one hand on each side of the door and propelled myself through, pushing off with my legs head first into the blast of 120 mph wind. I noticed that I seemed to be flying stably from the very start and that the head-first jump actually was easier because you could propel yourself clear of the turbulent air near the plane more quickly. My fears had been unwarranted.

From this jump on, my fear and anxiety were completely gone. I had passed through my biggest fear and found that in the end there was nothing to be afraid of. I had overcome my fear.

My perspective is the [rule] about removing fear (but I'd include any other emotion there) is most important. The reason is that you can only trade your beliefs. And beliefs that are not useful are easy to change if they are not charged with some strong emotion like fear. But if you have fear or any other strong emotion while you trade, then it is possible to charge limiting beliefs so strongly that they cannot be changed without professional help.

—**Van K. Tharp, Ph.D.**,
trading coach and author of the bestselling book
Trade Your Way to Financial Freedom

The Psychology of Fear

It is this aspect of my fears in skydiving that is most instructive to those who wish to understand the first of the seven rules for mastering risk: *Overcome fear.* The type of debilitating fear that comes with uncertainty and risk is fear that is triggered by threats. Like the snap of a branch, for most people in the modern world, uncertainty and risk trigger a set of primitive biochemical reactions that create a hyperalert state of mind often associated with anxiety. In some cases this anxiety can develop into a full-scale panic attack.

This debilitating fear makes it very difficult or impossible to think clearly. Overcoming fear is critical to being a successful trader, entrepreneur, or emergency room doctor because fear and anxiety impede normal judgment processes. Yet fear and anxiety are very common responses to risk and uncertainty. So, to be successful when confronted with uncertainty, you need to go through it to get beyond it.

For those who have anxiety and fear, this often seems like a huge obstacle. Fortunately, many people have learned to overcome their anxiety in trading especially, and the lessons we can draw from trading are very useful in business and emergency room medicine as well. In an article entitled "Emotions and Trading: Understanding Anxiety," trader and clinical psychologist Dr. Brett Steenbarger (author of *The Psychology of Trading*, Wiley, 2006) has the following to say about anxiety that comes from uncertainty and risk in trading:

> *Because trading involves risk taking in an environment of uncertainty, it necessarily engages us emotionally as well as intellectually. . . . we'll take a look at a family of emotional experiences related to anxiety. These include nervousness, tension, stress, fear, and worry. All represent a response to perceived threat. They are part of the "flight or fight" response that enables us to deal with dangerous situations.*

No two traders experience anxiety in the same way. For some, it is primarily a cognitive phenomenon in which thoughts become speeded up and worry sets in. For others, the cognitive component is joined with physical manifestations: a speeding of heart rate, tensing of muscles, and increasing of shallow breathing. . . .

Because anxiety represents an adaptive, flight-or-fight behavior pattern that is hard-wired, it prompts us for action. Regional cerebral blood flows engage the motor areas of the brain, bypassing the executive, frontal cortex responsible for our planning, judgment, and rational decision-making. For this reason, we can make decisions under conditions of anxiety that are not ones that we would normally make if we were cool, calm, and deliberate.

Notice that Dr. Steenbarger shows the dual cognitive and emotional response with anxiety. There is a visceral response with physical body sensations and a conscious response with thought working together to define our particular individual anxiety response. Now consider what Dr. Steenbarger says about the cause of anxiety:

Note that anxiety is a response to perceived threat. Such threats may be real, or they may be ones that we create through our (negative) ways of thinking. . . . It is not just reality, but our interpretations of reality, that mediate our flight-or-fight responses.

The two immediate challenges for traders experiencing anxiety are to become aware of the manifestations and to determine whether threats are primarily real or perceived. Knowing our unique manifestations of anxiety is invaluable in interrupting the flight-or-fight response and returning ourselves as early as possible to the cognitive state in which we can engage our sound, executive capacities.

So, in circumstances of uncertainty, our anxiety comes from two separate sources. There is the very real inherent threat that exists owing to the uncertain outcome itself. Then there is the perceived threat, which may be quite larger and which is a function of how you view the actual threat in your personal context. If you can change the cognitive context in which you place the threat, then you can change your perception of the threat itself and reduce your anxiety.

In the beginning, your fears from uncertainty are generally too high or too low because you lack sufficient context in which to frame them. When you have not even experienced the phenomenon yet, you only have your perception of the threat and danger owing purely to stories you have heard and the primitive emotions that come from any new and unknown stimulus. Some people don't have much initial fear, but they may develop this fear later after an accident or near-accident causes them to reevaluate their cavalier attitude. Others have too much fear, fear that reaches an irrational level.

As I became familiar with jumping out of a plane, I became less anxious. When I first jumped, it was hard to determine which of the many rules and lessons were the most important, so I had to view them all as critical until I got enough experience to make my own assessment. For example, in the very beginning, I was worried about achieving a stable fall so that the lines wouldn't wrap around me when the chute came out. Later, it became so easy to fly stably that I never worried about that aspect of skydiving at all. It ceased being any cause for anxiety whatsoever.

Refining Fear

We can decompose the fear and anxiety from uncertainty into three separate sources:

Novelty anxiety—the anxiety that comes from unfamiliar people, settings, or challenges.

Irrational anxiety—the emotional response and fear that go beyond a rational measure of the threat.

Inherent-threat anxiety—the anxiety that comes from a rational measure of the threat.

The task for the first rule for mastering risk is to refine your fear so that it consists only of that which is a rational response to the threat implied by the uncertainty. To do this, you need to reduce and try to eliminate to the extent possible novelty anxiety and irrational anxiety. Then, once the anxiety you feel is based *only* on the *actual* danger threatened, you can try to minimize the effects the presence of the *real* threat has on your decision-making process through the right kinds of practice.

Reducing Novelty Anxiety

The easiest type of anxiety to alleviate is novelty anxiety. This is the fear that comes from unfamiliar people, settings, or challenges. This type of anxiety tends to go away if you just keep doing whatever it is that is causing the anxiety. When you become familiar and competent in the new task or setting, the anxiety dissipates.

In domains where the anxiety can cause you to be a danger to yourself, you generally learn under the supervision of an instructor who is familiar with the mistakes made by beginners when they are afraid. In skydiving, this is the purpose of the initial training jumps. The instructors expect you to have a lot of anxiety. They are there to compensate for your likely poor performance because of this high anxiety. As this novelty anxiety lessens, a new skydiver is able to do more and more and generally becomes less and less anxious.

When learning to trade, you want to make sure that you don't lose all your money because of mistakes you make while you are trying to learn. Some start out paper trading, where they keep track of their trades on paper or with a computer spreadsheet, and determine how much money they would have made or won on a theoretical basis. This sort of simulated practice helps a bit too reduce novelty anxiety about the mechanics of trading. It does not, however, give you practice with the emotions of trading. There is no substitute for making real trades in a real market where there is a real risk of loss. New markets such as the Forex provide opportunities for new traders to trade while risking very small amounts of money on each trade. This allows a more realistic practice because the wins and losses, even if they are small, will help you to learn about your own emotional response to risk and uncertainty.

The presence of novelty anxiety is also one of the reasons that medical doctors are trained in residency programs. In a residency program, very experienced teaching doctors supervise new doctors. At first, the new doctors are watched more closely; then, over time, they lose their anxiety and require less direct supervision. The presence of the medical staff doctors helps to reduce the novelty anxiety so that patients are not put at risk because doctors are new to the practice of medicine.

Reducing Irrational Anxiety

Irrational anxiety is a little harder to overcome. Fortunately, there has been a lot of study of psychological phobia that is useful for those wishing to reduce their anxiety from risk and uncertainty. A *phobia* is an unnatural fear response in which fear is directed toward objects or situations that do not present a danger or present a minor danger and the danger is exaggerated in the sufferer's mind. Often the sufferer recognizes that his fear is unreasonable and seeks professional psychological treatment. Over the years, psychologists have developed therapies for phobias. Two of the better-known therapies are systematic desensitization (also called *gradual exposure therapy*) and flooding.

Systematic desensitization. Systematic desensitization is a process whereby patients are gradually exposed to the feared object until they develop a tolerance of it. Consider a patient with an irrational fear of spiders, even those that are not poisonous. Patients are first taught cognitive coping skills that will enable them to cope with more exposure to spiders than they normally can tolerate. This is necessary because the patients initially do not possess sufficient means for controlling their fear. Systematic desensitization therapy aims to help them build sufficient cognitive coping skills to completely overcome their irrational fear.

After they learn cognitive coping skills, the patients are gradually exposed to more and more of the dreaded spiders. First, they might be shown pictures of spiders. Then, after they can deal with pictures effectively, they might be exposed to a live spider in the same room in an enclosure. This might be increased to many spiders. Finally, they might touch live spiders. Between exposure sessions, the patient's cognitive coping skills are built to a sufficient level to enable him to handle the next successive exposures successfully.

Flooding. Flooding is a related form of phobia treatment that works by overwhelming the emotional response mechanism. Flooding does not involve developing cognitive coping skills. The basic idea is that the body cannot stay anxious forever, so by flooding the body with fear-causing stimuli, the patient eventually will feel calm again and realize that the fear-causing agent is not so fearful after all. The patient then even may begin to associate a feeling of calmness with the formerly feared object.

Coping with Fear of Uncertainty

Each of these therapies is instructive for those who have a fear of risk-taking and uncertainty. Systematic desensitization shows how developing cognitive skills, combined with gradual exposure, can be used to cope with anxiety, whereas flooding shows how repeated extreme exposure can lessen the effects of fear-causing stimuli. Both these therapies show that there is considerable merit to both the idea of practice and jumping in with both feet.

In another article on his blog, Brett Steenbarger talks specifically about how he would help a hypothetical trader named John who was having difficulty increasing his trading size as he made money because of the increased pressure and risk involved. For instance, John may have been successful trading a relatively smaller amount, such as a single contract of gold, but is too afraid to increase the number of contracts he trades so that he can make more money.

Here are Brett's comments:

You cannot rapidly change a pattern unless you face that pattern in real time. Talking about a problem does not, in itself, resolve that problem. People learn from new experience. John will feel comfortable getting larger by actually getting larger, not by discussing his insecurities. Accordingly, I might start John on a simulator and have him make some practice trades with larger size. I would teach him some basic cognitive and behavioral skills for staying calm and focused and encourage him to use those skills while placing his simulated trades. Once that goes well, we would raise his size just a small notch and have him trade live—again using the skills he's learned. Only when that's gone well do we ratchet up the size another small notch, and another, and another. John will internalize the repeated experience of success; over time, he'll think of himself as a larger trader.

These principles hold true whether you're working on trading discipline, marital arguments, or a fear of heights. Your work on yourself will be successful when you find a safe context to be the change you want to make. Changing by enacting solutions rather than discussing problems is a powerful way to develop yourself as a trader—and as a person.

Notice how Brett's therapy is very similar to the systematic desensitization therapy previous example for those with a spider phobia. Brett progressively exposes his clients to more and more of the stimulus that they fear until they are finally comfortable. The treatment for irrational phobias is similar to Brett's treatment for irrational fear in trading because our internal fear mechanism is the same whether our irrational fear comes from something physical or something in our heads when we consider risk.

The important thing to keep in mind is that we can overcome our irrational fears with practice and guidance. By slowly increasing our exposure to the feared object, we can slowly overcome our fear.

The Mind Killer

The reason that it is so important to eliminate irrational fear is because fear clouds the decision-making process. If it reaches a certain threshold, fear really is a mind killer. Fear causes you to pay extreme attention to your senses and depresses your ability to think rationally. Fear makes people avoid risks that make rational sense, and it causes them to take risks that they should rationally avoid.

Irrational fear is often what keeps otherwise very intelligent people from taking charge of their financial lives. Afraid of the uncertainty, some defer to so-called professionals for decisions on what investments to purchase for their retirement accounts because they are afraid of the uncertainty inherent in the decisions. Others make the "safe" choice because of the fear of uncertainty, one that may end up costing them thousands or hundreds of thousands of dollars over the course of many years because these choices result in low-return investments.

Irrational fear is what keeps people from selling stocks when they start to drop after having risen for years. It keeps them from buying stocks after they start rising again after several years of bearish markets.

Irrational fear is what drives the bandwagon effect. Some think: "Standing out is risky. You might be wrong. Everyone will know. Better to stand in good company. Better to join the bandwagon. Better to do what everyone else is doing before it is too late."

Irrational fear drives the public to invest at the tail end of a bull market when the rewards are thinnest and the risk gets fattest. In the beginning, they fear losing, so they stay out of the market. Then, later, when they see all the money their friends are making by investing, they fear losing out on the easy pickings. Finally, when the market turns and starts to descend again, they fear selling on the way down because they erroneously hope that the market will return to the highs.

While some people have less fear than others and so overcoming fear may come easy for them, many are naturally fearful. If fear affects you, I hope the conclusion to my story about jumping out of planes is helpful.

After about my eighth or ninth skydiving jump, I noticed that I no longer feared exiting the plane. When the fear cleared, I started to notice more. I noticed the ground down below and where the plane was positioned in relation to the landing area—called the *drop zone*. I noticed the clouds and the other skydivers who had jumped before me. I noticed the feel of the air on my body. I became a safer skydiver because of these things. I was less likely to inadvertently hit another jumper—which can be very dangerous. I was less likely to end up landing far away from the drop zone, where I might have to land in a hilly or rocky area and risk injury.

I also started to have more fun. In fact, after a few more jumps, leaving the plane and jumping out headfirst became my favorite part of the jumps. By facing my fear, I had turned that fear into joy. I also built confidence that I could face my fears and overcome them.

So face your fears. Look them in the eyes. Stare them down. Don't let them control you. Overcome them.

eight

ADAPT OR DIE

Water shapes its course according to the nature of the ground over which it flows; the soldier works out his victory in relation to the foe he is facing.

So a military force has no constant formation, water has no constant shape: the ability to gain victory by changing and adapting according to the opponent is called genius.

—Sun Tzu, from *The Art of War*

The single most important rule for mastering risk is to *remain flexible*. If you don't know what the future will bring, then you must be prepared for it to bring something other than what you expected. This point cannot be overemphasized.

It is not enough just to have a flexible plan. You must remain flexible. This means not painting yourself into a corner and not cutting off options for the future whenever possible. Remaining flexible is just as important as being flexible initially. Remember, the key to managing uncertainty is to be prepared for what actually happens. If you commit to a particular outcome and are unable to respond if the future turns out differently than that particular outcome, you will suffer much worse consequences than if you remain flexible and able to respond to the new circumstances.

Flexibility allows for greater adaptation and response to changing circumstances. Flexibility is especially important during times of rapid change and innovation.

Flexibility Drives Innovation

If one were to pick the single most important factor behind the dominance of U.S. industry in the world of the twentieth century, it would have to be the success of U.S. innovation. The telephone, electric light bulb, phonograph, moving picture camera, airplane, transistor, integrated circuit, mainframe computer, personal computer, and the Internet all were invented, developed, and turned into industry initially in the United States.

Perhaps the most important reason for the success of U.S. technology is not its inventors but its culture of innovation and the tremendous flexibility of the system of startup finance that enables it.

As a country of pioneers and immigrants, the United States is peopled by those who were willing to risk everything for a chance at a better life for themselves and for their descendants. Even today, thousands come from all parts of the earth with the hope of improving their lives. These immigrants come knowing that they will have to work hard so they can become economically viable. Those who are willing to do this are, almost by definition, risk-takers—the fearless, the adventurous, the "crazy" ones. The spirit these original immigrants bring is one of thoughtful risk-taking. This spirit informs America's culture, its politics, and its business.

General Motors versus Ford

One of the more interesting stories in U.S. business history is the story of the two rival major automobile companies of the twentieth century, Ford Motor Company and General Motors.

Most people know the story of Henry Ford, the great industrial innovator and founder of Ford Motor Company, who developed the system of assembly-line mass production, which has come to dominate factory work all over the world. Ford also invented the Model T, which stood for 50 years as the greatest-selling car model in history. With an 18-year run that started in 1909, the Ford Model T sold over 16 million cars. (It would not be until 1973 that the Volkswagen Beetle passed the Model T in total sales.)

In just the year 1924, Ford sold almost 2 million Model T cars. This represented over 60 percent of the entire automobile market for that year. But this success didn't last; 1924 also was the beginning of a precipitous decline in market share for Ford. By 1927, when Ford discontinued the Model T, sales had dropped to fewer than 400,000 cars and a 13.2 percent market share. In just three years, the number of cars sold by Ford dropped by 80 percent. The major reason for this drop was the rise of General Motors.

While most people know the story of Ford and the Model T's rise to fame, the story of how General Motors under the direction of Alfred P. Sloan overtook Ford and the Model T is far less well known. Alfred P. Sloan was one of the major innovators in the practice of management. His strategic insights at General Motors in the 1920s were key to General Motors passing Ford to become the world's largest automobile company.

First, in 1921, Sloan had inherited a company that was an amalgamation of several automobile companies that had been acquired by General Motors' founder William C. Durant. These companies included Chevrolet, Oakland, Buick, Oldsmobile, and Cadillac. Sloan streamlined operations and isolated the different divisions so that each division produced cars at different price points that targeted different groups of consumers. Chevrolet would market the most inexpensive cars and compete with Ford directly, Oakland (later to become Pontiac) built slightly more expensive cars, then Buick, then Oldsmobile, and finally, the flagship luxury cars would be produced by the Cadillac Division.

Henry Ford had his single model—the Model T—that had remained largely unchanged since its introduction in 1908. Under Sloan, General Motors would have tens of different models, each priced differently, and each with different designs and styling.

Sloan didn't stop there. The automobile industry was innovating rapidly. In 1922, Sloan's first full year of management of General Motors, the balloon tire was invented. This tire, now known as the *modern pneumatic tire*, offered a much softer ride than previous solid rubber tires did. Innovations such as hydraulic brakes, independent front suspension, safety-glass windshields, vacuum-assisted brakes, universal joints, shock absorbers, and many others that society now takes for granted were invented during just the first decade that Sloan managed General Motors.

Sloan instituted the modern practice of annual year model changes that have since become the standard in the auto industry. Each year the factory would shut down for a few weeks as the new innovations for that year were added to each car model. The higher-end models such as Cadillac and Oldsmobile had the newest innovations first. Then, as the price for any given innovation lowered as technology and production costs dropped, these innovations would be introduced in the lower-priced Pontiac and Chevrolet models.

In the 1920s, General Motors started to pass the Ford Model T until it became obvious even to Henry Ford that the days of the Model T were over and Ford needed a new automobile model. Even then, the benefits of Sloan's more flexible approach became obvious. Since the General Motors factories needed to retool each year to add improvements, the factories themselves were designed with flexibility in mind. The assembly lines had space around the machines so that if new machines required slightly more room, they could be accommodated.

Ford's huge River Rouge plant, which was built to make the successor to the Model T, in contrast, was so specifically tied to the new Model A that it was much more difficult to add machinery for new features later on. The factory could not support extensive annual model changes like the General Motors plants could.

Sloan's advances seem obvious today. He realized that General Motors could not reliably predict which features or models would be most successful. In some ways, each of the divisions and each of the individual models represented a separate experiment. The models that sold well would receive increased production resources. The failure of a single model would not endanger General Motors. By providing models at every price point and with different styling characteristics, General Motors was able to pass Ford to become the largest automobile manufacturer in the world. It has held that position for 77 straight years.

It has only been since the 1970s that General Motors has started to lose its dominance as it has given up the flexibility that was once its hallmark. Now you'll find Buicks and Oldsmobiles to be virtually identical. The spirit of experimentation and innovation that built General Motors has long since died.

Remaining Flexible

The key insights that Sloan implemented allowed General Motors to remain extremely flexible during a period of extensive innovation in the auto industry. This flexibility was the key to General Motors overtaking Ford so quickly. Ford, in contrast, bet the company on the single Model T and saw its market share drop by over 80 percent in the few short years between 1924 to 1927. Not learning from this mistake, Ford again came out with a single model, the Model A, to replace the Model T. This model sold well, but Ford would never again be the largest automobile company. The flexible company beat the rigid one.

You can learn the key principles behind remaining flexible from the early years of General Motors. When you don't know what the future might bring or what approach will work best, you should follow Sloan's example and

Experiment. It is better to try many approaches than just one or two.

Differentiate. It is better to try many very different approaches than many approaches that differ only in minor ways.

Adapt. Learn from what works, and continue to change and adapt your strategy as you find success.

Organize organically. Make sure that your plans account for the fact that the future will bring something you cannot anticipate.

Experiment

Sometimes it is necessary to choose one route and only one path and never divert from that route. Most of the time, however, this is not a wise way to proceed when you don't know what the future will bring. In that case, it is better to experiment with many approaches. Each of the models produced by General Motors was an experiment. Its sales were the results from that experiment. Sloan didn't know in any given year what would sell; he let the market determine that and only set out to make sure that General Motors would have a model that appealed to buyers no matter what the current trend.

Experimenting doesn't necessarily mean spending a lot of time on design process and running big market studies. Consider another story from the auto industry: the story of Lee Iacocca and the resurgence of the convertible.

In 1983, Lee Iacocca—who previously had been the successful president of Ford Motor Company before Henry Ford II fired him—was running Ford competitor Chrysler Corporation. Iacocca had been responsible for many successes at Ford, including the Ford Mustang. Iacocca felt that Chrysler needed some excitement. He wanted to introduce a convertible.

The combination of a concern for safety owing to Ralph Nader's book about the Chevrolet Corvair and very high gas prices had driven convertibles, or "rag tops," from the market over the previous decade. Cadillac sold the last convertible in 1977. It was hailed as "America's last convertible."

The normal process for introducing and determining market viability for a convertible would have taken months or years. Iacocca didn't want any of that. He had a new K-car sedan shipped to an auto customizer in California who turned it into a convertible and shipped it back to Detroit. Iacocca then drove it around as his personal car, doing his own market research based on the reactions he got. In his autobiography, he wrote: "I felt like the Pied Piper. People in Mercedes and Cadillacs started running me off the road and pulling me over like a cop. 'What are you driving?' they all wanted to know. 'Who built it? Where can I get one?'" On the strength of that experience, Chrysler built the K-car convertible and sold 24,000 cars in the first year, over eight times the marketers' estimate of 3,000 cars.

Differentiate

Running many different experiments, each of which is very similar to the others, does not remove as much risk as running many experiments in which each is intentionally different. Consider what Sloan did by creating stratification in the different pricing for each of the models. The stratification ensured that Chevrolet models would experiment with low-cost features, whereas Cadillac would sport expensive state-of-the-art features and design.

The differentiation also was a function of a decentralized control structure. Each of the divisions at General Motors had a lot of autonomy. This stands in great contrast to the divisional structure today. The autonomy resulted in greater differentiation and a more robust overall product line, as well as a stronger sense of pride and ownership for the employees of each division.

As the market for automobiles moved from the utilitarian Model T to a wider range of models built for different purposes, General Motors' sales continued to grow. Some of its experiments failed; perhaps most of them did. The ones that lasted were incorporated slowly into cheaper models as manufacturing advances made them more and more economical to produce.

Contrast this with the U.S. automakers today. They had become so heavily dependent on sales of expensive and heavy SUVs and trucks that they did not have the small, fuel-economical models consumers wanted after the rise in the price of oil and the threat of global warming. By concentrating their success on only one type of vehicle, General Motors, Ford, and Chrysler have jeopardized their very survival. They have not been able to adapt to the new market reality because they had not been running diverse experiments.

The more uncertain the business climate, the more important it is to run diverse and differentiated experiments. If the future turns out wildly different from what you expected, it may be that the crazy ideas save the day.

Adapt

The way that Sloan organized General Motors also made it easier for the company to adapt rapidly as the market changed. The adaptation was natural and gradual. Models that sold well were given sufficient resources in marketing and production so that General Motors could meet market demand as new niches in consumer tastes expanded. General Motors organized its financial controls and supplier relationships so that it could divert resources to divisions that were selling well from divisions that were not doing as well.

The important consideration here is that adapting does not require forecasting. It does not require that one know what the future will bring. It is possible to adapt in the presence of a large amount of uncertainty. The key is to pay attention to what the present moment is telling you about present ideas. Ideas that are working better than others provide information about the trend of movement in the external environment. Extrapolate from what worked in the near past to what works in the present, and you often can get the best guess as to what will work in the short-term future.

By feeding the ideas that are working in the moment and reducing the supply of resources to ideas that are not working, an organization can adapt successfully through significant change. This is the key.

Structure Organically

Sloan made sure that each of the divisions implemented identical financial reporting and control systems. This allowed General Motors to compare the strategies and effectiveness of each of the divisions and models. Ideas that worked well in one division then could be implemented in other divisions. General Motors oversaw each of the divisions by developing supply and financial systems to feed the requirements of each division. Growth came from the divisions and was supported by the central command structure. This was a bottom-up management style rather than the top-down one employed by Ford, where Henry Ford decided everything himself.

The General Motors model was more organic. Much like a tree growing in rocky soil, the growth in the root structure only happens when the soil is productive and where there is room to spread between the rocks. The tree strengthens the root system by expanding the width of the roots to conduct a greater amount of nutrients. The sections of the root system that grow more get a larger, thicker connection to the tree, and the sections that stop growing do not have their width increased. The tree feeds success and starves failure. This approach is the most flexible and the best strategy for operating in realms of high uncertainty.

The key insight is that this approach does not forecast what will happen so much as it responds to what is happening and what did happen.

I am an investor, a little bit of a trader, entrepreneur and angel investor...

I think [remaining flexible] is the most important rule for all my above interests and professions. Each time I get too focused on a particular way of doing things, I am at the verge of a major problem in business or loss in trading.

I think a lot about golf. The best players are skilled, but also flexible. The same hole they played yesterday with a driver off the tee may call for a 3 iron today. Wind, flag position, etc. all play a factor and you must be flexible. Likewise, in the market, conditions change all the time. Stocks can move from trending to chop in days and you must remain flexible.

—**Howard Lindzon,**
hedge fund manager, angel investor, entrepreneur,
and creator of the popular Web-based financial video
show *WallStrip*

Survival of the Fittest

In evolutionary science, the main concept first promoted by Charles Darwin was the idea of *survival of the fittest*. This may be a male perspective, but when I first heard this idea, I thought fittest meant strongest or healthiest. Over time, I have come to learn that this conception is wrong. The fittest animals from an evolutionary perspective are not the strongest, but those that are able to adapt most effectively to new circumstances.

Whether you believe that evolution is a process started by God or an inherent process of nature, there is no question that our earth has seen many different species come and go. The ones that have died off are those that were not able to adapt to new circumstances. They painted themselves into an evolutionary corner and were not able to escape. For example, one theory is that large dinosaurs required massive amounts of food so they died off when climate changes reduced the levels of food available.

You might liken this to the situation facing large SUVs in the United States, such as the Hummer or the Cadillac Escalade. Their use requires massive amounts of gasoline, which, in turn, depends on cheap oil in order to be economically viable for most consumers. This affordable oil was only available in the United States until recently, so it has been only in the United States that SUVs and large trucks were used as a primary means of transport. They were a niche product that relied on a very specific environment for their success. When that environment changed, they stopped being viable. They are phasing out, having reached an evolutionary dead end.

In the United States, investors like to look at simple measures such as quarterly profits and growth as sign of health. This measure is wrong in the same way that my teenage assessment of strength being the measure of fitness for evolution was wrong. The strongest organizations are those that are most adaptable. Those that deliver value and will continue to deliver products that buyers want, no matter how much consumer tastes change and no matter what the outlook for energy prices and global warming costs.

Consider the current economic crisis. Many large financial institutions stand on the brink of bankruptcy and failure. The reason for this is that they took on too much risk in the form of collateralized debt obligations (CDOs) and convertible debt swaps (CDSs). They painted themselves into a corner. They took on obligations that were so large that their liabilities swamped their considerable assets. They, too, became like the dinosaurs, fragile and vulnerable to small changes in the external environment.

A relatively small change in the default rate of certain types of mortgages, something that should have been part of company contingency plans all along, has taken down some of the biggest names in Wall Street. These big banks were vulnerable because they did not remain flexible.

The measure of the health of an organization should not be how much it is able to squeeze out of the current circumstances, but rather how likely it is that it will continue to be able to provide value in the future. Over the next several decades, one thing is certain: There will be changes, major changes. The uncertainty associated with modern life is increasing. If you want to survive, it is critical that you remain flexible and ready to adapt to whatever those new circumstances bring.

The age of the megadinosaur is over. The age of the smaller, warm-blooded, more adaptable mammal has begun.

RISKING RIGHT

The greater danger for most of us lies not in setting our aim too high and falling short; but in setting our aim too low, and achieving our mark.
—Michelangelo

When I was 19 and inducted into the Turtle Program, I and my fellow Turtles were trained for two weeks in December 1983 in the methods of our mentor Richard Dennis (who we all called Rich). During the training, two points were drilled into us over and over.

First, don't overtrade. Overtrading means using too much leverage by trading too many contracts. Rich and his partner Bill showed us how the risk of going broke while trading increased exponentially after you reached a certain optimal trading size. He also showed us a specific method for determining how many contracts to trade in each market. Fortunately, if we followed Rich's method, we didn't have to worry about overtrading. He provided us with strict limits so that we could avoid this common problem.

Second, during the training, Rich kept emphasizing the importance of not missing any trends. As Turtles, we looked to make money from large market moves. Missing a trend meant watching the market move without buying to take a position. For example, if you bought 100 contracts of gold on the Comex commodity exchange, you controlled 10,000 ounces of gold because each contract specifies 100 ounces. So, if gold went from $400 per ounce to $1,000 per ounce, you have made $600 per ounce times the 100-ounce contract size times the 100 contracts for a total of $6 million in profits. If you didn't buy any contracts, you didn't make *any money at all.* In Turtle parlance, you "missed the trend."

The reason that it was important not to miss the trend is because there might only be two or three big trends each year. If you missed out on a particular trend, this could mean the difference between making 50 to 100 percent returns and losing money. One big trade could represent all the profits for the whole year. So those were the two biggest takeaways from the training: Don't overtrade, and don't miss the trend.

During that two-week training, we were taught two very specific trading strategies, we called *system one* and *system two.* These two strategies were very closely related. Each of the two strategies held the idea in common that we were to buy contracts in a given commodity when it reached a new high price. System one directed us to start buying when the price exceeded the high of at least 4 weeks; system two, when the price exceeded the high of 11 weeks. For both strategies, we were told to buy in four chunks—which we called *units*—the first unit when the price exceeded the high and the following units after the price moved a bit further. Both these strategies outlined very specific rules to ensure that we never missed a trend.

So we were given two primary mandates: Don't overtrade, and don't miss a trend. We also were given specific rules for trading that would ensure that we didn't violate either of these mandates.

After the training ended, we had a brief vacation over the holidays. We returned in early January 1984 to start trading. Rich said that we would be judged according to our trades for January and that he would give those of us who did well a $1 million trading account. He gave us each two trading accounts, one for system one and one for system two. We were to trade these accounts for a trial period that would last at least until the end of January. To make the process simpler during the trial trading period, we were told to make each unit a fixed three contracts for every commodity we traded.

We also were told to write down in a notebook the reasons we made every single trade. These could be as simple as "Bought gold at $400 because it exceeded the 11-week high." It would have been pretty easy for someone to just follow the orders of another trader even if they didn't understand what we had been taught. To prevent this, Rich wanted us to explain our rationale behind each trade so that he could figure out if we each individually understood the training.

During this first month, January 1984, the price of heating oil rose to the point that both our trading strategies, system one and system two, indicated a buy. In the case of heating oil, its price exceeded the 11-week high of $0.8450 per gallon. So, according to the rules we were given for both system one and system two, we should have started buying our first unit when the price got to $0.8451.

After the price went up a bit more, according to our instructions, we should have bought additional units until we reached the maximum four units we were permitted. For the training period, Rich supplied trading sheets each Monday that indicated how much price movement was required for putting on each additional unit. For heating oil, these trading sheets indicated that we should buy after each $0.0050 per gallon price increase. So we should have purchased the second unit at $0.8501, the third at $0.8551, and the fourth and final unit at $0.8601.

Not only did heating oil go up past the $0.8601 mark, it went all the way up to $0.9800 within a just a few days. According to any reasonable interpretation of the rules we were given, we each should have purchased all four units; therefore, we each should have had 12 contracts of heating oil in our trading accounts. The rules that prevented us from missing a trend indicated that we should have bought all 12 contracts.

All 12 of us Turtles sat in a medium-size room perhaps 30 feet by 20 feet with six rows of two desks each. The room was without any partitions for the trial trading period — the partitions arrived later. So we could easily overhear each other's conversations on the phone with the order desk. I expected that we would all handle the trading in a similar manner. I expected that our results after the first month would be virtually identical.

Now, just to be clear again, I could see no possible interpretation of the rules we had been given that would have resulted in a purchase of anything less than all 12 contracts. So imagine my surprise when I found out that not only was I the only trader among the Turtles who had bought all 12 contracts, but many of the Turtles had no position in heating oil whatsoever, not six contracts, not three contracts, but none, zero, nada.

The difference between my view and those of the rest of the Turtles came down to one simple thing: We saw risk and danger in different places. The Turtles who skipped the heating oil trade were worried about losing money. I wasn't. I knew that Rich understood that losing was part of trading. He knew that we'd have to risk a loss to put ourselves in a position to win big. I knew that Rich would rather see us follow the rules we had been given than not follow them, even if it resulted in our losing money.

Rich understood that just having his money actively traded involved significant risks. So he expected his money to be working for him. He told us two things: First, don't overtrade, and second, don't miss a trend. The first rule made sure that we didn't lose too much of his money if the market turned against us; the second rule made sure that we didn't miss out on making him money. If we followed his rules, I felt that he would reward us. I thought that the riskiest move of all would have been to not enter a trade after a market started moving and thereby risk missing a major trend.

As it turned out, I was right. When it came time to hand out the real account sizes after the January trial ended, a few traders received a $1 million account like we had hoped, a few others received a $500,000 account, and many were told to keep trading using the smaller trial-period three-contract units. Rich handed me the largest account, $2 million. From February 1984 on, I traded the largest account of any of the Turtles. Rich made this assessment almost entirely as a result of the questions and answers we had in the two-week training class and that first month of trading. I believe that how we handled the heating oil trade was the single biggest factor in Rich's evaluation and therefore the single biggest factor in our personal earnings over the next four-plus years.

Sometimes not risking big is the biggest risk of all.

Taking Reasoned Risks

Many people equate risk with danger, the potential for harm or even death. For them, risk is something to be avoided whenever possible.

This way of thinking is wrong. You cannot avoid risk. Risk is inherent in any human activity and indeed in life itself. Risk is necessary, even vital to progress and advancement.

So the trick is to understand the risks that you do undertake and to make sure that the risks you run are reasonable when one considers the alternatives and the potential rewards from a given course of action. This is the key idea behind the third rule for mastering risk: Take reasoned risks.

This rule is active. You need to take risks. Running risks is good for you. You won't learn and you won't accomplish anything of merit if you do not take risks. So part of applying this rule in our lives is the requirement that you actively consider risks, you think about them, and you decide to take them. You make risks part of your life so that they become intentional acts rather than happenings that seem to come from outside you and over which you have absolutely no control.

The rule is also a warning. People tend to be of two different minds when it comes to risk: They take on either far too little risk or far too much risk. Striking the right balance is both hard and uncommon.

In my opinion, the most important rule in relation to the field of venture capital is to "take reasoned risks." Life is unpredictable and you are always acting on imperfect information. You can never avoid risk, but you can do things to manage it, i.e. skew the odds in your favor.

Generally speaking, the ways that venture capitalists manage risk can be divided into two categories: procedural and substantive.

Procedural risk management involves integrating a series of procedural safeguards into your investment process in order to ensure that you don't let passion for an idea or company overcome reason.

Examples of procedural safeguards include:

1. *Having a clearly articulated set of investment criteria*

2. *Having a strict investment process*

3. *Forcing fund partners to justify any deviance from the criteria or procedures*

4. *Scaling into an investment (funding in tranches)*

5. *Tying the funding of tranches to the meeting of milestones*

6. Requiring sponsoring partners to clearly articulate exit strategies for perspective portfolio companies prior to making an investment, etc.

Substantive risk management involves an analysis of company-specific issues. Examples of substantive risk management would include:

1. Only backing serial entrepreneurs

2. Only backing teams that have worked together before

3. Avoiding seed-stage companies in favor of companies that already have working products or services

4. Only investing in companies that are already profitable or at break-even

5. Investing in companies that have an "unfair advantage," such as a patent position that allows them to dominate a field

6. Only investing in companies with low burn rates and short roads to profitability that require small upfront investments, etc.

By "taking reasoned risks," venture capitalists can improve the odds of success while minimizing the odds and severity of losses.

—Simon Olson

Balancing Risk

While avoiding risk at all costs is a problem and can result in far less success in any endeavor, taking on too much risk can mean financial ruin or death. There is a reason that you fear the unknown and uncertainty. It may not be wise to let your fears rule your life, but it is just as unwise to ignore danger and act as if nothing can harm you.

So the key to the third rule for mastering risk is to maintain an intentional balance between too little risk and too much risk. One might liken this control of risk to the control of speed by the accelerator pedal on a car. If you press down too hard and don't let up, you are much more likely to hit another car, a pedestrian, or a fixed object such as a tree or telephone pole. If you don't press down hard enough, you will find that you don't get very far, that you travel too slowly. There is no "safe speed" that one should always travel.

The trader's equivalent of that accelerator pedal is the financial concept of leverage. Just as a mechanical lever such as a big stick can help you use a small force to move a heavy object, financial leverage can be used to increase the power of an investment. For many homeowners, the mortgage loan they get from a bank is a form of financial leverage. If a homeowner places 10 percent down on a $200,000 house, that loan provides 10:1 leverage. A $20,000 down payment plus the $180,000 loan from the bank allows the homeowner to control $200,000 in underlying assets. This means that if the housing market goes up only 10 percent, the homeowner's equity in the house will double in value. If the home rises to the value of $220,000, that leaves $40,000 in equity after the $180,000 loan to the bank is accounted for.

Leverage increases the amount of money that can be both *won* and *lost* when investing. In recent months, many homeowners have seen the downside of this leverage. Anyone who bought a home with 10 or even 20 percent down at the housing market peak now may be facing the loss of their entire investment. Consider the home bought for $200,000 with 20 percent or $40,000 down. If the market dropped 20 percent, that home is now worth only $160,000, the same amount as the loan. By the time you factor in selling commissions, the original $40,000 investment is completely wiped out, and the homeowner will end up paying to sell the home.

For many people, perhaps most, the equity in their home is their largest investment. A loss of this equity owing to a downturn in housing prices can devastate a family's financial planning for years. This is the reason that it is important that anyone who is considering an investment understands the impact of leverage. Markets go up, and markets go down. To think that you will always be lucky enough to invest in a rising market is to tempt fate too much.

For stock investors, U.S. law allows only limited leverage. Using what is known as *margin accounts*, investors may borrow up to twice the amount they put into their account for use in purchasing stocks. In this way, an investment of $10,000 in a margin account can be leveraged to purchase up to $20,000 in stocks.

Leverage in the stock market, as everywhere, can be a two-edged sword. I have several friends who made small fortunes in the stock market Internet craze in the late 1990s only to lose everything back when the market declined in 2000. A decline of 50 percent in the value of a stock will result in 100 percent loss of the investment if the stock was purchased using the full 2:1 leverage allowed under U.S. law for a margin account.

One of the most popular new trading vehicles is the trading of foreign currencies in what is known as the *Forex market* (*Forex* is short for *foreign exchange*). At the institutional level, foreign-currency trading is the largest market in the world. Trillions of dollars worth of currencies are traded every day in these markets. Most of this trading occurs between big banks on behalf of global corporations.

More recently, smaller retail Forex brokers have opened, allowing smaller traders to trade in the same types of markets as big companies, hedge funds, and investment banks. These retail Forex brokers offer very high leverage, sometimes as high as 100:1 or 200:1. This leverage can be very dangerous to new traders. Using 100:1 leverage, for example, it is possible to buy $150,000 dollars worth of euros for $1,500. This means that if the euro goes up 1 percent against the dollar, the investment of $1,500 will double. Conversely, a decline of 1 percent will result in complete loss of the $1,500 investment.

Yes, pressing the accelerator pedal down to the floor can be fun and exciting. It also can be very dangerous if you don't know what the road ahead will bring. Don't let yourself be seduced by the potential winnings made possible by high leverage. High leverage can be as dangerous as it is lucrative if you are not careful.

Risk Management for Traders

The difference between a trader and an investor is a matter of perspective and expectations. Generally most investors—especially nonprofessional ones—expect to make money on each investment. They focus on the positive outcomes, the returns they will get, the appreciation they expect from their investments. Traders are different; they expect to lose money on their trades a significant portion of the time. Traders understand that losing is part of the game and that you can't expect to win on every trade. They understand that uncertainty keeps them from being able to do so.

Successful traders understand that uncertainty can bite hard at times, so they often focus on the negatives outcomes. Rather than thinking about how much money they are going to make, they think about how to keep their losses minimized in the event that their trades turn out poorly. They think defensively.

Since successful traders pay great attention to risk, many great traders have written about the importance of risk management. For this reason, many beginning traders spend a lot of time on *risk management* or on a phrase borrowed from gambling theory, *money management*. Both these terms refer to the systematic control of leverage. For most traders, risk management is simply a function of controlling the amount of money at risk in aggregate at any one time. For commodities traders, this generally means controlling how many contracts one buys; for stocks, the number of shares one buys.

Entire books have been written on money management in trading. Since trading involves buying and selling at particular prices, and since prices are numbers, there is a tendency toward an overemphasis on formulas and mathematics in the trading literature. Some have proposed simple rules of thumb such as, "Risk 2 percent on every trade." So some traders have proposed complex formulas for deciding exactly how much to trade. Many believe that this complexity is necessary and valuable when dealing with risk.

The truth is simpler.

The formulas tend to obscure the truth about risk. What makes risk difficult is the underlying uncertainty. This uncertainty never arrives in a predictable manner. If a particular outcome is reliably predictable, there is no uncertainty. Remember that the fundamental problem with uncertainty is that you don't know what the future will bring. You don't know because the future is uncertain.

I keep coming back to this simple and seemingly obvious idea: *When something is uncertain, you don't know what will happen.* In so many areas there is a strong tendency of people of all types to forget this.

When you don't know what will happen, *you don't know*. No amount of formulas or theory or complex rearrangement of the parts will change this fundamental fact.

Unexpected Catastrophe

For most traders, the real danger lies not in going too fast, from having too much leverage in normal circumstances. The danger lies in the occurrence of *an unexpected catastrophe*, a large, unexpected adverse price movement, one that happens so quickly that there is no way to avoid the associated losses. In finance, these are often called *price shocks*.

Recently, trader and author Nassim Taleb has popularized these movements with the term *black swan*, which means a high-impact sudden and unpredictable event. The most recent example of a black swan is the September 11, 2001 terrorist attack on the World Trader Center and the Pentagon. It didn't really matter where you might have wanted to sell your stocks on September 11; when the market opened up a few days later, the price was much lower, and there was not much anyone could do about it.

The only way to reduce the risk from price shocks or black swans is to intentionally reduce the leverage of your trading so that you have less exposure to underlying market movements. Remember that risk is defined as exposure to the consequences of uncertainty. By controlling their use of leverage, traders can reduce the risk they incur. This can mean the difference between having a bad day and losing everything.

One example from my days as a Turtle stands out in particular. In 1987, the fourth year of the Turtle Program, I was trading a $20 million account for Rich. In early October 1987, I was short Eurodollars and other interest-rate futures. I had the maximum number of contracts allowed according to Rich's rules. This meant that we made money when the price of the Eurodollars went down. So for me at that time in Eurodollars, down was good, and up was bad. Eurodollars had been going down, I had been making money for months, and my total profits were on the order of $12 or $13 million. This represented about 65 percent profits on the year, a respectable but not great year for us Turtles.

Then came the stock market crash of October 19, 1987. Since I wasn't trading any stock market futures, the day of the crash itself didn't affect me much. I even had a small profit.

It was the next day that killed me. The U.S. Federal Reserve reacted to fears of another potential Great Depression by causing interest rates to drop overnight. This erased my entire year's profits before the next day's market open. Before that open, the Eurodollar went up more than it had dropped in the previous six months. So I lost the entire 65 percent profits overnight.

Relative to many others, I was okay. Sure, losing all the earnings for an entire year was no fun, but at least I hadn't lost more than my winnings. Had I been trading at two or three times the number of contracts, I would have been down $10 to $20 million on the year. That would have made for a really bad day.

Now, there was no magical formula that I used to make sure that I didn't lose too much because there is no way to predict ahead of time exactly how much money a given price shock or black swan will cost or even if you will be beneficially or adversely affected by such a shock. Risk is like this. That's because uncertainty really is uncertain.

Real-World Safety

As much as it might be nice to use a specific formula to be able to arrive at a risk level that has mathematical precision—for instance, a 1 percent or less chance of a loss of more than a 30 percent drop in value—

the real world is not this precise. There is no magical formula because the future is not reliably predictable.

What you can do is look at the big price shocks in the past and see what might have happened if they were to occur again, and then you can use that information to make an informed guess about the likelihood of a particular bad outcome in the future. Here's how you might do this. For our example purposes, I'll assume an investment account of $100,000.

Let's consider a few of the biggest single drops in stock market history. First, the 1987 Black Monday stock market crash. In one single day, the market lost over 20 percent of its value. If you had money invested in stocks or mutual funds, you would have lost around 20 percent of the value of your investment. If you had money invested in a margin account at 2:1 leverage, you would have lost 40 percent of your investment that day.

Here is where the danger of leverage will become evident. If you had instead bought S&P 500 Index futures contracts, you could have purchased 10 contracts using just half your $100,000 investment (i.e., $50,000). By doing this, you would now control contracts that fluctuate in value to the same extent that $1,300,000 invested in shares of the stocks in the S&P 500 Index stocks would have. This represents 13:1 leverage. So a 20 percent drop in the price of the underlying index would mean a loss of $260,000. So, if you had been trading futures, you not only would have lost your entire $100,000 investment, you also would now owe the broker an additional $160,000.

Now consider another huge price shock. If you invested $100,000 in American Airlines stock on the close on September 10, 2001, you would have lost 46 percent of the value of that stock before the market opened on September 17, the first day of trading in the American stock markets after the September 11 bombing. There was no opportunity to trade between those dates.

More recently, an investor who had purchased $100,000 in Bear Stearns stock at the closing price on Thursday, March 13, 2008, of $57.34 would have watched that stock drop the following day, March 14, to a close of $29.99, a drop of 47 percent in a single trading day. The next Monday morning, on March 17, that drop would reach 95 percent as the price dropped below $3.00 per share.

Using any of these three price shocks as a template, it is possible to make guesses about the likelihood of a similar scenario in the future. If you are investing in a broad-based index fund or mutual fund, it wouldn't be unreasonable to expect to see a 20 to 25 percent drop in one day. It has happened once before. If you are investing in single stocks, they can conceivably lose nearly all their value in a single day. This has happened many times in the past, and almost seems to be a weekly occurrence in the current 2008 financial crisis.

For most people, a loss of 20 to 25 percent of their entire investment account is a terrible blow. Yet many people have all their money invested in stocks and mutual funds, where these sorts of drops are not at all uncommon. These people are not taking reasoned risks. They are risking too much.

You Can't Hide

The most damaging types of risk are those that can be attributed to common wisdom or accepted practice. These risks are hidden behind the veil of conventional wisdom, but they are still there. They are damaging because most people do not understand the extent to which they are exposed to very real possibilities for loss.

Consider the common buy and hold strategy for investing in stocks. This is the strategy that mutual funds are mandated to use by federal law. Buy and hold strategies keep you in the markets at all times. Anyone using a buy and hold strategy saw their investment value dip from 35 percent to 40 percent in just the year 2008. A buy and hold strategy carries significant risk. You are exposed to the full risk that the market will drop in value.

Portfolio managers are stuck with rules that say they have to be 95 percent invested or more. This means they also cannot practice risk procedures that would protect them in really bad markets and this is why most retirement portfolios are being wiped out.

The public at large is told to buy and hold. There are many years in the last 100 that if you bought and hold for 20 years, you'd be unlikely to make any sort of substantial return. For example, right now we're in a secular bear market and these tend not to end until the S&P 500 pays dividends of around 5 to 6 percent and has a single digit PE ratio... and we're a long way from that right now.

The public at large is told that market timing [entering and exiting investments rather than buying and holding] is a fool's game. This is because the people who talk about market timing don't understand the principle for risk to reward in a trade; they don't understand cutting losses short and letting profits run; and they don't understand what super returns people could get by just missing the worst market days.

—Van K. Tharp, Ph.D.

If you have an investment in a mutual fund then you are at risk for losses. Stock markets are not magic. There is no reward without its concomitant risk. There is no free lunch. So you need to consider the risks you run very carefully. If you want to earn higher potential returns, then you will have to expose yourself to the possibility of higher potential risk.

First do no harm (primum non nocefere) is a useful perspective in assembling the prospective constellation of right responses. The human body has a strong propensity for self-healing, while an investment portfolio does not.

—Bruce Tizes, M.D.

Risk Is Personal

The process of deciding exactly how much risk to take on at one time is a personal one. Too many people look to formulas and rules of thumb, or they defer to the advice of so-called professionals without really sitting down and thinking about the ramifications of a particular course of action or even understanding what it is that they are investing in.

If you invest in something, you will be the one who lives with the results of that decision. If you let someone else define your tolerance for risk, you may end up with an outcome you don't like.

Many people deferred to the experts during the 2008 financial crisis and held their investments in stocks and mutual funds as they watched them drop by as much as 35 to 40 percent (if they were lucky). If this sort of outcome is not acceptable to you then you must learn how to be your own expert.

So, instead of deferring your risk control to others, I suggest that you take control of your own life. Spend more time reading about past problems. Spend more time thinking about how the future can go wrong and what you are going to do about it. Don't let someone else tell you how much risk is too much or too little. Doing so likely will keep you blinded to the very real risks that do exist or keep you from taking those risks that others deem too great but that might suit you just fine.

THE RIGHT WAY TO BE
WRONG

*A wise person adapts himself to all contingencies; a fool struggles
like a swimmer against the current.*
—Unknown

Acertain comfort with one's own limitations is a universal sign of
maturity. After you have been around long enough, you stop thinking of yourself as invincible or infallible. You lose that teenage bluster.
You stop trying to pretend to be anything other than what you actually
are: a fallible person capable of both good and bad, not privy to the right
answers all the time. You also stop trying to prove that you are correct
all the time and even grow comfortable with the idea that you might
be wrong, even wrong about some of your most carefully guarded
assumptions concerning what is important and how the world works.

Even when you have achieved a level of personal maturity, when you
step out of your personal sphere into the larger social ones, you find that
people are not so advanced when working as groups. As communities,
cities, states, and a global society, group behavior is less obviously
mature. Groups are less sure of themselves, and at the same time, they
have a greater need to hide their mistakes, to rewrite history as if none
were made, and to pretend that they won't make any in the future.

This approach is wrong. Societies should study their mistakes. Leaders should publicize them far and wide. Citizens should expect their leaders to make mistakes in the future. And most of all, society should learn from what works and what doesn't when confronted with similar situations in the future. Finally, society and groups should not let the fear of making the wrong decision prevent them from taking a course that may have risk of failure.

Fear of Failure Drives Decisions

One of the more interesting differences between rapidly innovating companies such as technology startups and mature companies is the way they approach the decision-making process. Small companies are more concerned with *getting to the right answer* quickly. Bigger companies are often more concerned with *avoiding the wrong answer.*

A small company will gather all the relevant decision makers into a room, and they will talk things over and come up with a plan. That plan becomes *the plan* for the moment. During the discussion, there likely will be certain known issues or obstacles that the group will know may cause the plan to fail. During the meeting, there likely will be alternative ideas or ways of approaching the problem that may take more time or money or involve more risk of failure. These ideas will become alternatives should the main plan fail. In a small company, the plan is the plan—until it is not.

Team members in a small company don't expect that the plan will never change; in fact, they know that it most likely will. Changing course is relatively easy, and for this reason, choosing a course is also easy. Since less time and effort are put into the specific plans, team members tend to be less personally invested in any particular plan. So the costs of switching plans are relatively low by comparison.

A large organization, in contrast, makes decisions slowly, by a deliberate process. The decision makers generally would rather someone else make the decisions. The actual act of choosing in a big company or government bureaucracy is all risk and little reward. You are expected to make the "right" decisions. If you do, it rarely matters. If you lead a group that makes the wrong decision, however, you can put an indelible black mark on your record that can affect your career for years.

In small organizations, the goal is to make the best decision. In large organizations, the goal is not so much to make the best decision as to avoid the wrong decision. This is one of the reasons why the decision-making dynamics of large organizations stifle innovation. Consider a company faced with choosing among three suppliers of software technology for supply-chain and inventory management:

Elite Software, Inc.—software with high ratings used successfully by many companies, but that is very expensive.

Cheapo Software Corp.—software that many companies use and that costs one-tenth the cost of Elite Software's technology, but that everyone agrees is basically unsuitable for the problem at hand.

Innovative Software, LLC—software that everyone agrees is the best fit for the problem, is the most likely to work and also costs one-tenth the cost of Elite Software's technology, but that has not yet been used by any leaders in the industry.

From the company's perspective, the best choice is Innovative Software's product. Interestingly, there is almost no chance in most organizations that a team charged with choosing among them would make a choice for Innovative Software. The problem is that what is good for the company is not good for the individuals' career aspirations.

Most likely, there will be a fight between finance and the representative of the employees of the department that will need to use the technology—in most companies, this will be called something like "operations." The finance people will argue for Cheapo Software because it represents a big savings. The users in operations will opt for Elite Software, arguing that spending money on Cheapo Software will be a waste because it does not meet their needs. So the company will either spend too much or buy a product that probably will not meet its needs.

So why does the product from Innovative Software not get the consideration it should?

In large organizations, *following experts or others who have done similar projects* is not wrong, even if it does not bring the intended benefits. Doing *what has always been done* is never wrong. Doing *something new* may be. This is a key difference.

Consider the three alternatives from the perspective of how they might affect one particular decision maker's career: John Reynolds, vice president of operations. Here are the possible outcome scenarios:

Elite Software

- **Best case** (most likely): The system works well, and users are happy. The decision makers do not lose because the financial impact of the expense will not be attributed to them.

- **Worst case** (least likely): The software doesn't work for some reason. This will be blamed on the team implementing the software within the company because the decision makers will be able to point to success at other companies using elite software.

Cheapo Software

- **Best case** (least likely): The system works well, and users are happy, so there is no one to blame, and everyone is happy, even the CFO.

- **Worst case** (most likely): The software doesn't work for some reason. This will be blamed on the user representatives. John will be blamed as their head.

Innovative Software

- **Best case** (most likely): The system works well, and users are happy, so there is no one to blame, and everyone is happy.

- **Worst case** (least likely): The software doesn't work for some reason. This will be blamed on John and his team because they chose an unproven product. John will not be able to point to other successful implementations at other companies. John will not be able to pass the buck. John will have sullied his career.

So even though Elite Software's product represents more risk to the company because it will be spending more money for a solution it doesn't think is as likely to work, John will pick Elite Software. He will not be blamed if it doesn't work. He will not be responsible for the high costs. He will not be held responsible if the CFO overrides his vote and chooses the cheaper products. His safest vote is for the proven but expensive solution.

This kind of dynamic plays out in most large organizations. There is very little incentive to take risks and very little reason to stick one's neck out. This is why most large organizations do not take the lead in innovation. They put so much time and effort into making a decision that they believe they cannot afford to be wrong.

A better approach, in this instance, would be for the company to negotiate with both Elite Software and Innovative Software to implement a pilot project. Rather than trying to make a decision before there is enough information—an approach that will force the company to the least risky option, the company should acknowledge that it doesn't know and run a real-world test with both products. If the solution from Innovative Software works, the company will have a lower-cost solution and potentially a better fit. If it doesn't work, the company can continue to implement the solution from Elite Software.

Preparing to be wrong is not a defeatist or pessimistic perspective. It is simply a humble one. It is one that acknowledges the unpredictable nature of uncertainty. The fourth rule for mastering risk, to prepare to be wrong, advises that you behave in a manner consistent with having come to grips with your own infallibility.

The key elements of the fourth rule for mastering risk are

- **Be wrong early.** If possible, try to develop your plan so that you will know as soon as possible if the plan will fail.

- **Be wrong often.** When operating in uncertainty, you need to try many different approaches and continue to feed the ones that seem likely to work.

- **Diversify the risk.** Unless there are overwhelming reasons to choose only one route, spread the risk out over many different vehicles.

Wrong Early to Be Right Early

The decision to go with a newer and possibly better approach, but one that is less proven, is one that software developers often face. Many software companies face this choice when working on major new projects. Often there is a lot of contention between the more conservative members of the team, who want to use proven ideas and technologies, and the more adventurous members, who want to try a new idea or new technology.

Rather than force an either/or decision, it is often possible to start down the path of first determining whether the new approach would work or not, while reserving the more tested approach as a backup plan. A failure of the new idea will not place the project in jeopardy *if found out early enough* to redirect the team's efforts.

This is *a very important idea*. In this case, having things not work out is within the scope of the plan. The plan would be to try design A long enough to see if it is going to work and then to switch to design B if you eventually find out that design A will not work. By scheduling the work appropriately, it is most often possible to perform the critical testing up front so that you can finish your project on time in either case. So, rather than waiting until the tenth week of a 12-week project before starting work on a critical piece of technology that you know might not work as planned, you should do that work in the first few weeks. This will leave you with sufficient time to use an alternate design and keep the project on schedule if the hoped-for design doesn't work out.

Sometimes there is no clear answer, especially when venturing into a new area where your team does not yet have much experience. In cases like these, many people spend a lot of time trying to figure out which way forward will be best. Often there is insufficient information at that point to make any such assessment. For this reason, it is often better to rapidly choose one path. Then, in the process of proceeding, you often learn enough to make other decisions as you are going forward. When doing this, expect that you might change your mind and that you are simply using the first choice to learn enough to better understand future issues.

The important consideration here is that *when you don't have enough information to make a good decision, there is no point in wasting time in the decision-making process.* You need to acquire more information. You need to learn. You don't learn by deciding; you learn by doing and thereby succeeding or failing. As long as everyone is aware that the decision is tentative and exploratory, then it should be easy to change course if it becomes clear that another alternative would be better.

So don't be afraid of making hasty mistakes. Often the best way to get to the right decision is to quickly make the wrong one while remaining open to the possibility that you will need to change course.

Always Have a Plan B

In some respects, operating in uncertainty is a bit like trying to escape from a complex labyrinth. You have to go down one of the corridors in order to figure out if it is a good path or not. The key is keep track of the paths you have taken so that you don't revisit routes that you already have determined do not lead you anywhere.

Even when trying to solve a complex maze on paper, most people don't expect that their first attempt will lead them to the solution. No, they expect to hit a few dead ends. They know that the process of solving the problem will require a bit of trial and experimentation. Likewise, when dealing with uncertainty in your business life or financial ventures, you should conduct yourself in a manner that is consistent with having come to grips with your own infallibility. You might be wrong, so you should set your expectations and plan accordingly.

If you know that it is likely that the future will bring things you don't expect, then it makes sense to have alternate plans. You need to have a plan B; if you are smart, you will have plans C, D, E, and F as well. Instead of spending your time worrying about whether or not plan A or plan B is better, you often would be far better off if you simply picked one and then monitored your progress to make sure that you are still on the right track. As long as you remain unsure that the current course will work out in the end, you need to have a valid and well-thought-out plan B ready to go.

In larger organizations, it may be possible to start plans A, B, and C all at once, and then at some future point you can evaluate all three strategies and eliminate any if they are not working as well as the others. Optionally, you can replace one of the failed plans with plan E or F when it becomes obvious that one of the plans won't meet the goals of the project. For organizations that don't have the resources to fund multiple plans at once, having a plan B handy if plan A doesn't work out can save months of time and avoid having a small problem turn into a huge one.

The Wonder of Diversity

Another excellent way to prepare to be wrong is to follow the old adage, "Don't put all your eggs in one basket." In investing, this is also known as *diversification*. An investor diversifies by moving from one investment to many smaller investments. This brings two important benefits. First, it reduces the chance that one bad event will affect the entire portfolio of investments; second, it reduces the importance of the decision-making process for choosing an investment. Both these benefits reduce the risk of the investment portfolio without normally reducing the returns from that portfolio.

Consider two investors: John and Mary. John puts his entire $100,000 retirement fund in the stock for Acme Computing, the company where he works. Mary splits her $100,000 retirement fund among 25 different stocks. Mary also happens to have $4,000 invested in Acme Computing. If there is a sudden 50 percent drop in Acme stock because of a patent infringement suit by a larger company, John will have lost 50 percent of his entire investment, or $50,000. Mary will have lost only 50 percent of her $4,000 investment, or $2,000.

So John loses half his money, and Mary loses only 1/50 of hers. This is one of the benefits of diversification: A bad event affects a diversified portfolio far less than it does one concentrated in only a few investments.

> *Diversification is as close to magic as we can come; however, diversifying by the purchase of inferior assets is detrimental to overall portfolio return.*
>
> —Bruce Tizes, M.D. J.D.

A Net versus a Hook

Now consider the other major benefit to diversification: the reduced requirement for precision during the decision-making process. You could liken a diversified approach to casting a net over a wide area, whereas an undiversified approach is like fishing with a single hook. If you fish exactly in the right spot, you can catch fish with a hook just fine. If there are a lot of fish, a net cast over a wider area gives you a better chance and makes success more likely.

Suppose that you are a partner in a venture capital firm, Venture X, and you have allocated $10 million to invest in new green technology companies. If you invest all the $10 million in the right technology, you will make the most money. In most industries, though, the distribution of wealth does not come evenly. The number one company generally earns most of the money, whereas second earns considerably less, and after the third or fourth in a given domain, the other companies may lose money. So, if you invest all $10 million in one company, you better be right.

Consider 10 technology company investments that might end up with the following annualized returns after three years:

Company	Return
A	150%
B	70%
C	30%
D	20%
E	10%
F	−100%
G	−100%
H	−100%
I	−100%
J	−100%

If you are an investor who wants to invest in this segment of the technology industry, you could pick one company, and you might end up with the winner and get a 150 annual percent return on your money, or you might end up with the second or third player and wind up with a smaller return. Or you might end up with one of the losers and watch your investment disappear.

So how does diversification help?

The key is noticing that the important factor is not avoiding losses but making sure that you have company A and B in your portfolio. If Company A returns 150 percent for three years, that means that the it returns more than 15 times the investment. For company B, 70 percent would return almost five times the original investment. If you divide up the $10 million and invest $1 million in each of the ten companies, on average you would end up with 2.1 times your original investment for an average annual return of 28 percent. So even though five investments result in a complete loss, on average Venture X would obtain an excellent return.

In addition, in many cases, it is easier to tell a bad idea or see the signs of a poorly run company than it is to pick a winner. Picking the exact winner is complicated; you need to compare the relative benefits of various strategies and evaluate the capabilities of a management team in an industry that you might not follow too closely. But, if you could eliminate just two of the bad companies that you believe will go broke, then you will do even better. Instead of making 28 percent, you end up making a 42 percent return. You do this not by being able to pick the winner, but by eliminating a couple of the losers.

If you really know which company is going to win, then diversification is not required. If you don't, it can help a lot. So, when you don't have a lot of expertise picking the best investment, diversification is a good strategy. The higher the level of uncertainty, the more diversification helps.

Even the most seasoned venture capitalists understand the benefits of diversification. Many of them will not invest with a company without bringing in one or two other firms. In turn, these other firms will share their investments so that these investments are pooled and result in greater diversification. Each firm getting to invest in two or three times the number of deals that they can each handle individually.

For most investors, diversifying by picking individual stocks is too much trouble. Fortunately, the financial services industry has created prepackaged products that make diversification easy. Investing in a mutual fund is one way for an investor to easily diversify without significantly complicating the process of investing. In most brokerage accounts, it is just as easy to purchase shares in a mutual fund as it is to directly purchase shares of a single company.

Making Peace with Not Knowing

A consistent theme of this book and my advice for handling risk and uncertainty is coming to grips with the reality of the unknown. This is the fundamental core of uncertainty: You just don't know what will happen. It seems to be very difficult for many people to face this simple truth.

The belief that the future is more precisely knowable than it really can be is at the heart of a lot of wasted time, money, and human effort. So stop pretending that you know what you don't. Make peace with uncertainty. Keep a plan B ready in case you are wrong. Try two or three different approaches instead of one. Diversify your investments in ideas, people, and companies.

Making peace with uncertainty brings one further benefit: It makes it far easier for you to face reality when it does come. But that's a subject for Chapter 11.

REALITY BITES

Reality is not always probable, or likely.
—Jorge Luis Borges

As a trader, there is nothing in the world more important than an accurate picture of reality. The best traders have the best perception of reality. They have the best information networks—both computer- and human-based—and they understand the indescribably complex set of interconnections that places specific values on each individual item of information.

For pure price traders, sometimes known as *technicians*, finding reality is relatively easy. The current price in a given market represents the reality of that market. It doesn't matter what she thought might have happened or what she wished would have happened, the price represents what is happening right now. To the technical trader, price is reality.

In the early 1980s, when I first learned about trading, the state-of-the-art trading setup was a satellite feed hooked up to a specialized computer system that would allow you to see the price of the markets with a delay of perhaps 5 to 10 seconds from the action on the floor. Clerks employed by the exchange sat just outside the floor, relaying prices to the exchange's electronic price feeds. These prices, in turn, would be sent via dedicated phone lines to the satellite uploading centers, where they would be relayed to customers throughout the world.

These systems cost from $300 to $500 per month for up-to-date quotations of the current prices. In the mid-1980s, most traders used systems that displayed only the prices. There were no charts showing the pricing over the course of the day, like the ones traders commonly expect today. These sorts of graphing systems were just starting to come to market, and only a relatively small percentage of traders used them at the time.

Traders know that their decisions sometimes will result in losses. They also know that they need to know about those losses as soon as possible. A focus on what the market actually does—the market's reality—keeps successful traders from burying their heads in the sand and pretending that the world is other than it actually is.

Dealing with a Fuzzy Reality

Traders have it easy. You can make one phone call or Web search to find out how much crude oil someone can sell next August and at what price. You can ascertain the market with a pretty high degree of certitude; many tankers' worth of oil can be negotiated in seconds.

Reality can be a much fuzzier concept for entrepreneurs and startup investors. Consider a technologist who has an idea for a new product that he thinks might have a market and a marketing guru who has an idea for a product that she thinks will sell well. Their ideas represent an educated guess at the state of reality, but those guesses may not be correct. In fact, they may be widely off mark. The technologist may overestimate the market for a product because he does not understand the potential buyers well enough. The marketing guru might underestimate the difficulty of building the product she believes will sell well or the price at which that product can be built using today's technology.

The potential mismatch between their educated guess and reality defines the uncertainty in their collective decisions. For the typical venture, there may be hundreds of these educated guesses. The collective uncertainty of all these educated guesses combined with the investment contract defines the total risk of the venture from the venture capitalist's perspective. For the entrepreneur, typically everything is on the line.

In medicine you have to start with the worst-case scenario. What is the worst thing that could be wrong with this person? And work your way down from there. Likewise with trading, you have to ask yourself: Am I willing to do this trade knowing the worst that could result? In medicine, you need to be able to handle the extremes. If someone comes in and you think to yourself: "I'm going to have to open his chest. I can handle the issues." Then you are ready to face whatever happens from there from the worst case backwards. If you find yourself thinking: "It's probably only this or that minor problem," you will quickly be in over your head if the worst case turns up.

— Ted Patras, M.D.

Actively Seek Reality

This chapter covers the fifth rule for mastering risk: Actively seek reality. For traders, this means getting accurate information as quickly as you can. For most traders, reality is easy to find.

For most people engaged in other enterprises, reality is *not at all* easy to find. So the important factor is that you must actively seek for that reality—*search for it, dig for it, hunt for it, and pry it up even.*

Reality isn't like some benevolent old uncle who drops by when you haven't been paying attention to say, "Have you considered that your competitors have twice tried to enter this market and failed, losing millions each time? Have you looked into the reasons why it is that they failed?" Or perhaps, "You know, it might be wise to ask the engineers how much it would cost to build this product before selling it to the customers at $X."

Human beings are so very skilled at confabulating explanations for a particular condition or result. Thinking upon information at the least granular or highest level where certainty exists is an essential condition precedent to any correct analysis. Emergency physicians who believe, in the absence of evidence, in an incorrect intervention plan injure their patients. Similarly, traders who believe they are right and the market is wrong injure their portfolio.

—Bruce Tizes, M.D.

Crash Landing

In a startup, there will be mistakes, plenty of mistakes. Sometimes, though, you get so close to success that you can count on one hand the mistakes that take you down. These are the ones that hurt, the ones where "if only" haunts your sleep for years to come.

I remember one time I was preparing for the marketing launch of the first major product of a new software company I started a few years after the Turtles Program ended called *Borealis*. At Borealis, we wanted to create a product that was much more flexible, much easier to customize than the products provided by my competitors. We had been thinking about the types of innovations for the product for years, so many of the best engineers from previous companies joined this new effort. We also set out to get some outside investment so that we could build a first-class startup team.

At Borealis, we had one of the finest software engineering teams ever assembled, one as good as the one that built the first Macintosh or the first version of Photoshop or Microsoft Office. One of the reasons that I was able to build such a great team is that I myself had been programming since I was 16 and, in honesty, am probably a better software architect than I am a trader. Further, I had been selling tools to software developers for the Macintosh at my company, Sierra Software Innovations, for five or six years, so I got to know some of the best software developers in the business.

At the time that the Turtle Program disbanded, all the best programmers developed for the Macintosh. Even the best Microsoft programmers were Mac programmers; the team that developed and released the first versions of Word and Excel did so on the Macintosh. So, luckily enough, I knew programmers from many of the world's best programming teams on a first-name basis.

By the time of the product launch, all of us at Borealis had spent two years raising money, building the team, and writing the code for the first product. It was ground-breaking technology that was even better than my initial dreams and hopes. It was technology that could support the company for years to come. The development team was justifiably very proud of what we had built.

The software allowed you to develop complex data applications by dragging and dropping. Where our competitors required you to write code, we did the work automatically. Our philosophy was that if there were a task that it was possible for the computer to perform instead of the programmer, then our program would handle the task automatically instead of requiring the programmer to write code. At the same time, we provided the flexibility to allow for programming different behavior so that there were no limits to what our customers could create with the software.

Ten years after the company died, the software would still be state of the art in several respects; it was that innovative.

Among other things, our software did what no other software at the time could do well—manage remote clients. In the days before high-speed Internet, most corporate salespeople used dial-up Internet connections. Where today they would use an internal Internet site to let salespeople access sales data, in those days, companies had to rely on custom software that ran on each laptop.

Keeping track of the data and software configurations on each of those laptops was an IT nightmare. Our software made this job much easier. We also did it much faster. Some competitive products required salespeople to remain online for as much an hour each day downloading updates. Our product typically could accomplish the same work in two or three minutes.

Finally, we could send changes to the software itself, so our customers could easily update the software on each of the laptops without requiring salespeople to bring it into the home office. We believed that the combination of these key features would help make our product the market leader in just a few years.

We were wrong.

The moment I first realized that our perspective was seriously flawed (or I should say *my personal perspective* because I can't speak for the rest of my team) came at the beginning of a major press tour. For those of you who have never been on a major product launch, a press tour involves three weeks of travel visiting the major industry press and independent pundits and advisors (groups such as Gartner, Inc., and its one-time rival the Meta Group, who advise companies on their IT strategy) ahead of the actual announcement so that they had time to write announcement articles or, in the case of the pundits, so that they could advise their clients about our products.

This launch was a big event for us. It was the culmination of five years of dreams and two years of solid hard work. At the trade show, we would announce our product to the world. It was our big coming-out party as a company and as a product in the sales automation field.

We weren't ready.

We were wrong in several important ways, any one of which could have independently jeopardized the company. First, we were marketing a product rather than a solution. Companies pay to have their problems go away. They don't buy software because it amuses them. They buy software to fix existing problems. We should have been marketing our product as a solution to specific customer problems. Our ads, our PR effort, everything should have been targeting solutions to specific problems.

Second, we had a sales team that was not used to making complex sales to senior management. Our assessment of our sales progress in many accounts was pure fantasy. This was not because anyone was making forecasts up; I believe that our team believed the numbers they provided. The problem we had was that our sales team had no experience selling to the types of buyers that bought our software—vice presidents of sales, CEOs, and CFOs for major international corporations. The software they had been selling looked very similar to what we were now selling, but the people who bought the software were of a different makeup altogether.

Third, our software team had built the best tools possible for creating sales solutions but no actual solutions. Our product would let you quickly build solutions to problems, but it came with no good solutions out of the box. From a prospective customer's viewpoint, it didn't do what the customer wanted.

This last mistake was a huge blunder, and this particular blunder was entirely my fault. I was the head of the company, but I didn't yet have a vice president of engineering, so I was directly responsible for the product itself because I was one of the major architects, and all the development staff reported to me. I had not been paying enough attention.

We were gearing up for our product launch, and I had been spending time preparing the marketing launch. I was working directly with my marketing communications manager and PR agency preparing the publicity tour, which was set to consume the three weeks before the public product launch. The launch was to take place at the major sales automation exposition of the year (it would now be referred to as a *CRM exhibition*—CRM stands for *customer relationship management*). That particular year, it was being held at the convention center on Navy Pier in Chicago.

So, while my attention was elsewhere, I had not been attending the engineering meetings where the schedule was discussed and where the status of the features was discussed, and more important, I had not been there to see for myself how things were going. I had a world-class team of developers, and I trusted them with the product and the future of the company.

I was wrong. Not because my team wasn't trustworthy, but because the team had been subtly changing the definition of *done* to meet the deadline we had set. This was standard practice for a good engineering team that had a fixed deadline (such as a big industry exhibition or trade show). Normally, I would have been at the meetings watching this happen, so we didn't have a formal process for advising me of these changes. The changes were so gradual that I'm sure that team members didn't realize how much they had dropped or what had been dropped. Looking back, I'm sure that team members thought I knew what the status of the product was because they were not trying to hide anything and were all working extreme hours to meet our schedule.

The problem was that the key features that had been dropped out of the product were seen as minor features by the developers, but from a marketing perspective, they were essential. Since the developers were not marketing people, they didn't realize this. I was the crucial link between development and marketing, and I failed.

Further exacerbating this problem was that I had set expectations—that we were ready—with the outside world and my board of directors and the investment bank that was handling our public offering. If I had known earlier, I could have set proper expectations as to our real status. Now we looked like vaporware sellers to the outside world, I looked like a poor manager to my board of directors, and the guy who was handling our offering at the investment bank, Patrick Grady, thought I was a liar who had known all along that we were significantly behind schedule. He had sold a deal to his investors based on a different reality, and he rightly blamed me for the mistake. He was wrong about my being a liar, but I can understand why he thought that I was, and he was right to blame me for his having to go back and tell his potential investors that things were not as rosy as he had previously thought in Borealis land.

Patrick was instrumental in our landing two excellent additions to our board of directors: Ed Esber and Joe Marengi.

Ed Esber was one of the original high-technology rock stars. He was responsible for the marketing strategies for VisiCalc, the world's first spreadsheet, and had been CEO of Ashton-Tate (the makers of dBase) during the time when it was the largest software company in the world, and he had served on the board of directors for Quantum, Inc., the world's largest disk drive manufacturer at the time.

Joe Marengi was senior vice president of the Corporate Business Group at Dell Computer, Inc.; prior to that, Joe worked as chief operating officer (COO) at Novell, Inc., the makers of CP/M, one of the first cross-platform operating systems for early PCs, and the makers of Netware, which was once the most popular networking protocol— before the Internet and TCP/IP took over the world. Joe was one of the two finalists considered for the CEO position when Ray Noorda (who had been CEO of Novell for 12 years) retired. The other finalist was Eric Schmidt, who went on to be CEO of Sun Microsystems and who is currently CEO of Google.

Our vice president of sales, Rick Mellor, helped me to bring in Peter Pitsker for the board. Peter was the founding CEO and president for Wonderware. Wonderware was one of the high-tech darlings at the time. It completed its initial public offering (IPO) a few years earlier and had a market value over $500 million at the time Pete joined—in the days before the Internet boom, that was a really big market cap for a new company. Pete was an all-around great guy who had lots of senior sales experience.

Since we were based in Incline Village, Nevada, at the time, a small town located on the north shore of Lake Tahoe and 200 miles from the Silicon Valley network, I felt that our ability to attract to our board of directors such experienced and successful executives meant that we really had a shot at success. They served to confirm my gut feeling that our company was something really special.

Things were going pretty well until we hit another bump in the road.

The Seasoned and Green Legal Team

One of the big names in the high-tech world is the law firm of Wilson, Sonsini, Goodrich, and Rosatti (known in the valley more colloquially as Wilson Sonsini or WSGR). This company is known as the best legal firm in Silicon Valley, and it has offices in Palo Alto, New York, San Diego, San Francisco, Seattle, Shanghai, and Washington, DC. We had been damned lucky to get the firm to take us as a client.

Our attorney at Wilson Sonsini was Steven E. Bochner. He is extremely bright and a very nice guy. He is one of the best high-tech lawyers in the country and has taken many huge high-tech companies public. He has taught courses at the UC Berkeley School of Law and Stanford Law School and has been a guest instructor on venture law and business issues at both the Stanford Graduate School of Business and the UC Berkeley Haas School of Business. Some of Steve's other clients included Applied Materials, Inc., Autodesk, Inc., Genentech, Inc., Goldman Sachs & Co., and Sequoia Capital, many of the biggest names in Silicon Valley and the world.

So we were really lucky to have an attorney as good as Steve in the top firm in the world for high-tech startups handling our IPO. I was about to do my first IPO, and Steve would be my guide. Doing an IPO consists of two things: (1) writing the prospectus, which is submitted to the Securities and Exchange Commission (SEC) for approval before you are allowed to sell shares publicly, and (2) the road show where you go out to sell investment bankers on your company so that they will advise their clients to buy the offering.

I found out pretty quickly that the IPO process consisted mostly of group writing, a complete nightmare. Imagine 10 to 15 people sitting in an enormous conference room writing a 35-page document that is supposed to both excite and scare potential investors at the same time. The process is essentially a sentence-by-sentence fight between company management and the investment bank on the one hand and its respective legal and accounting teams on the other.

My management team consisted of myself, my head of sales, Rick Mellor (who was also a big investor and instrumental in many key hires and the acquisition of several board members), and my long-time friend Tim Arnold (who was an incredible jack of all trades and managed to teach himself accounting sufficiently to take us public as the CFO, all while running Borealis operations).

Borealis management and Patrick from the investment bank wanted the prospectus to be sexy and attractive to entice investors, and the legal and accounting teams wanted to protect us from shareholder lawsuits by ensuring that the prospectus warned investors of every possible risk imaginable (seemingly including the risk that a meteorite might possibly hit our headquarters).

The legal team included Steve Bochner, our seasoned veteran, who was a senior partner at Wilson Sonsini, and two associates who did the grunt work of writing the prospective. Our associates each had degrees from Stanford Law School. One had perhaps three years' experience, and one was a pretty fresh graduate. This arrangement was typical and made perfect sense. There is no way that we could expect an attorney with as much talent as Steve to sit there for the two weeks it took us to write the prospectus. He had other clients, and we only needed his advice when there was a controversy or when an issue fell outside the expertise of our associate team.

We spent one entire week of 16-hour days working on the prospectus at the office of Wilson Sonsini and another week at the financial printer, where they had sophisticated software for keeping track of changes to pages (this was before the days when Microsoft Word had these features) so that we could make revision after nit-picking revision with ease and precision.

On the last Friday, the day we expected to finish, at about lunchtime, the more senior associate took me aside and warned me that he thought Patrick was going to be hostile and try to get me replaced as CEO. This didn't really surprise me because I knew that Patrick was hot because our product wasn't ready, which meant that revenues would not come in as quickly, which meant that an investment in Borealis carried higher risk, which, in turn, meant that our IPO would fetch a lower price and potentially be less attractive.

The senior associate proposed that our legal agreement with the investment bank include a provision preventing the bank from mounting a proxy fight to change out the board of directors. A proxy fight essentially means mailing a package out to each of the stockholders advising him or her that you are seeking to propose a board of directors that is different from the board proposed by management. This is usually done with the purpose of removing senior management afterward. I told the young associate that I thought there was no chance Patrick would go for including the proposed provision but that he could ask Patrick's attorney if he wanted. I warned him that in no possible way should he present this as a deal breaker. The deal had to go through, and I was willing to run the risk of a proxy fight. Besides, I figured that Patrick would calm down after we worked together for a while. Then I kind of forgot about the conversation.

About 14 hours later, we finally finished the prospectus and chose to present it to the printer as the final copy that would be submitted to the SEC. After two weeks of 12- to 14-hour days, we we're finally done.

Since we were done, I told everyone I was going out to check my voice-mail messages and call home. I came back into the room about five minutes later, and Patrick was livid; he told me the deal was off, walked out of the room, down the hall, and left the building. His attorney, who had worked with him on many deals, told me that Patrick was very serious and that he didn't think we could salvage the deal anymore.

I was wide-eyed and wondering what had happened while I was out of the room making phone calls.

Both the associates' faces were ghost white. They took me into another room and told me sheepishly that they had chosen the time I was out to ask Patrick's lawyer about the provision against a proxy fight. Patrick thought I had put them up to it and had picked the late hour thinking that he would not back out after putting so much time into the deal. Patrick was wrong, but he was understandably livid about the timing, and given what he assumed, he had just cause to call off the deal.

The associates were very surprised that I wasn't angry with them, but I had been there myself; lack of experience leads to poor decisions at times simply because of the lack of some specific necessary information. They had done something very stupid, something that very well might bankrupt their client, all of us at Borealis. Rick was really upset and blamed Wilson Sonsini for what he saw as malpractice.

I didn't hold Wilson Sonsini liable or see it quite that way myself. I had approved the conversation. I was completely aware of the lack of trust on Patrick's part. I should have simply told the more senior associate "No" when he proposed asking for the anti–proxy fight provision. I knew Patrick wouldn't go for it; there was no point in even asking. It was a mistake on my part as well. I never in my wildest dreams would have imagined that the associates would have timed the question so poorly, but I couldn't blame them for doing what I had clearly approved.

They both thought the deal was definitely dead. This would effectively mean that we would be bankrupt because we had been raising expenses in anticipation of the deal going through, and we had no backup plan. I thought I could save the deal and told the associates as much. I called Patrick over the next several days and managed to salvage the deal by agreeing to have two directors leave. This balanced the power between inside directors who favored management (and me) and the outside directors. This balance of inside and outside directors would ensure that the management at Borealis served the investors' interests in addition to our own—for example, by not overpaying ourselves with salary and stock option grants, among other things.

This change in the board makeup effectively meant that it was much more likely that the board of directors would fire me if I screwed up again. In effect, I had to give up control to save the company. One of the directors who I had to ask to step down was my friend and fellow Turtle, Mike Cavallo, who had been advising me and had been a board member for quite some time, and the other was my father. Calling them and telling them that they would have to leave were two of the most difficult tasks I have ever had to perform. My father was heartbroken, and I'm sure Michael felt shafted; he had invested a substantial sum in the company precisely because he was on the board of directors and he would be unable to sell his shares for a full year because of the IPO. I had let a friend down and felt terrible.

A year or so later, the new composition of the board would result in my losing control of the company. Patrick himself eventually took over the CEO position. Another year or so after that, Borealis was bankrupt, with a stock value of zero.

My having not paid close attention to the reality of the product status started a cascade of events that caused me to lose control of a company that I had worked eight years to build and to eventually lose virtually my entire investment. At the same time, the power struggle between Patrick and me, which grew out of his distrust of me, caused us to lose the real fight with Siebel Systems, which grew to be valued in the billions over the next several years. Tom Siebel kicked our ass while Patrick and I fought over the company's direction.

Not paying attention had cost our investors the potential for billions. If only . . . I had actively sought reality.

twelve

ACT IN TIME

*It is even better to act quickly and err than to hesitate until
the time of action is past.*
—Karl von Clausewitz

I have worked with a lot of different startups and groups when they
were in the middle of a major decision. Invariably, many in the
group are confused about their proper role and indeed the role of the
decision itself.

In conditions of high uncertainty, which includes almost all decisions made in startups or rapidly changing industries, a decision always
defines the next step in a series. It does not define the endpoint because
in conditions of high uncertainty, everything is tentative and likely to
change in the future. That five-year marketing plan that everyone
spends so much time on typically won't last more than six months. It
will get updated and changed as you gain feedback from customers and
competitive products come online.

Therefore, much of the focus on getting to exactly the right decision
or the perfect model of the future is misguided and perhaps even dangerous because it wastes time. Often, time is the most precious resource
for a startup that is trying to survive and grow until its revenues exceed
its expenses, the so-called breakeven point.

When Time Matters

One of the more ironic truths in human progress is that sometimes the quickest way to find the right approach is to choose the wrong approach quickly. We discussed this in a previous chapter, but it is relevant here as well.

In software development in particular, I have found that decisions requiring the consensus of a large group of people are most often quickly resolved in the following manner: Split the teams into two groups, and have them each work on their preferred approach.

This means that you might have one team working on the "faster" code, whereas the other team is working on the safer, more traditional route. If the faster code is not ready before you need it, you may have wasted a few weeks of time in engineering. However, you may have saved

On September 11, 2008 we woke up to some fairly sour news regarding Lehman Brothers. Though we were not long the equity we did have some small positions in the bonds in some of our institutional accounts. We had to call around the street to get bids on the bonds which were anywhere from 72–74 cents on the dollar. Part of our sell decision is to ask ourselves, "in possession of today's news would we initiate a new position in a distressed Lehman at 72 cents on the dollar?" My partner and portfolio manager Matt Rogers pointed out that using simple math, there was 30 cents of upside if Lehman survived. There was 72 cents of downside if they failed. We hit the bid, sold the bonds, and Lehman announced bankruptcy the next day.

—**Niall Gannon**

an equivalent amount of time by avoiding an argument with all the hard feelings and sense of betrayal that come with losing or, worse, putting the project at risk because the team tries the faster code approach and doesn't finish in time. Having no plan B, the safer traditional route isn't started until far too late.

When time matters you need to act quickly.

In all areas where decisions are made in circumstances of high uncertainty, time matters. Traders need to get out of the market quickly when it turns against them. Entrepreneurs must respond quickly as their perception of reality changes. Doctors need to administer treatment while there is still time.

Another example from Borealis will serve to illustrate the importance of acting while there is still time.

Borealis Self-Destructs

My last year at Borealis was painful. I sat mostly on the sidelines watching as a series of new CEOs made decisions I wouldn't have made, and the board delayed in taking actions that needed to be taken much more quickly. I felt like an outsider in a company I created, and soon I would be completely out the door. Patrick convinced the board that I had been "shopping the company," or trying to find a buyer for it. I had been doing no such thing, but I had mentioned to a couple of the oldest employees that I thought that doing so was our wisest course.

After our initial product launch, we had a 12- to perhaps 18-month window in which to start selling vigorously. We had missed that window. After about a year or so, the competition could make two separate but lethal claims: (1) If our software was as good as we claimed, we should be selling more, and (2) our sales were not covering our expenses, and we would soon be out of business without a significant influx of capital. To a big company that could not afford to purchase mission-critical software from a company that might soon be out of business, it was the second claim that was most damning. It was true, and it was killing us.

In our initial public offering (IPO), we had raised a bit over $12 million, which was enough to last us about 12 to 18 months at the then-current rate of expenditure (known in the industry as our *burn rate*). After a year of dismal sales, we required more cash because no large company would buy from a small company that had only six months' cash in the bank. So we decided to raise another $6 million in another public offering, which would provide us with enough cash that companies would buy from us. We did this twice while I was still there. Each time we did this, our chances for success grew smaller. Our competitors' stories would continue to gain strength if we did not make significant sales.

There was some irony in our sales at this point. We had four major customers: Northern Telecom (later Nortel)—at the time the largest mobile sales automation installation in the world, Nortel would later become one of the Internet darlings because it manufactured the networking equipment used by many telecom companies to implement the Internet's fiberoptic backbone; SynOpSys—a provider of computer chip designing software; Maersk Line Shipping—one of the largest container shipping companies in the world; and Heidelberg Printing Machines—the largest global manufacturer of printing presses. These were all major corporations with global sales organizations. But two of these customers, SynOpSys and Nortel, predated our going public; they were a result of (1) our having the best Macintosh product on the market and (2) the work of my sole salesperson and me selling face-to-face. Maersk Shipping came from the relationship that one of our system integration partners, American Technology Corporation, held with Maersk.

So, with $18 million spent on growing our organization (the bulk of which was spent on sales and marketing), we had *only one new account* to show for it. We had done better when Rick Mellor and I sold it ourselves—before we had a sales organization. And so, at what would end up being my final board meeting, I told the rest of the board members that I felt *we should sell the company.*

I didn't know it but Patrick had wrongly informed them in advance of the meeting that I had been trying to sell the company behind the board's back.

This was not true. Even though I thought it was our best option, I had not made any attempt whatsoever to sell the company or even hint to outsiders that we were considering this. Nevertheless, the board was sufficiently angry so as to not listen to what I had to say. Deciding whether to sell a company and at what price is definitely the prerogative of board of directors in any company, especially a public company. Had I been doing what Patrick accused me of, the board would have had good cause to be angry. But I hadn't, and the board's decision to ignore my advice was costly.

Fewer than two years later, I heard through the grapevine that management at Borealis was trying to sell a significant portion of the company to Cisco. It was too late. Something must have fallen through in the end, and the deal was canceled at the last minute.

There was a time to act. And we at Borealis had missed it. Borealis' investors, customers, and employees paid the ultimate price when it ceased operations and declared bankruptcy.

Icarus Falls Again

After Borealis imploded, my plans changed. With the drop in stock price to near zero, I could no longer afford to pay my own personal expenses while working on building the management team for a new startup I had been planning. I could no longer afford the flights around the country and other associated expenses. I needed to get a job.

Finally, after I thought about it for a while, I realized that this was a blessing of sorts. One of the problems I had while CEO of Borealis was that I was disconnected from the pulse of Silicon Valley. Even at the time, I didn't realize how essential the networking of Silicon Valley is to a budding high-tech business. But I had seen through a couple of phenomena that I was missing out on something important by being so far away. So I decided to target my job search to include companies in Silicon Valley.

For most venture capitalists, if you weren't in the valley, you weren't serious. It was just that simple. We could talk about how much easier it was to recruit engineers to live in the mountains, but in the end, they never believed us. How could they? They knew something about the Valley that I didn't at the time. It had a life of its own.

So, at the height of the Internet craze, I decided to descend into the belly of the beast.

A headhunter kept calling me about a job at a new company called Icarian that really seemed to fit my skills and background well. Since Borealis had failed primarily because we couldn't get our sales and marketing effort off the ground in time, I wanted to find a software company with the opposite problem—one with really smart sales and marketing executives that needed help in their engineering department. I wanted to learn first-hand how a first-class sales and marketing organization worked. I found such an organization at Icarian.

Icarian was run by Doug Merritt. Doug was young, charismatic, smart, connected, and an almost beloved CEO. People really liked Icarian and working for Doug. Icarian's mission was to improve the world by helping companies make better hiring decisions. Better people mean better companies. That was the idea.

At Icarian, I worked as a consultant to the product marketing organization helping them with a redesign of their major product. After a couple of major success under my belt at Icarian, Doug tried to get me to join the company full time. I really liked the people there. It was a

The Omen of Icarus

Icarian was great fun to work for. The name was fun and sounded good. But if you were familiar with the Greek legend of Icarus and knew how he met his end, the name seemed a strange one.

Icarus was the son of Daedalus—the master craftsman of Crete. Daedalus was commissioned by Minos to build the labyrinth used to imprison the minotaur. Minos later exiled Daedalus and his son, Icarus, after Daedalus assisted Minos' daughter, Ariadne, in thwarting the labyrinth. Ariadne gave her lover, Theseus, the secret to kill the minotaur and escape using a ball of red string to keep track of his entry path.

Daedalus—being the master craftsman that he was—was not easily outfoxed. Minos controlled the sea around Crete so Daedalus decided they would escape by air. He built two pairs of wings made from wax and feathers, one for himself and one for his son Icarus. Daedalus warned Icarus not to fly too close to the sun because the heat from the sun would melt the wax. Icarus did not pay enough attention to his father's warning and flew so close to the sun that the wax in his wings melted and he fell back to earth and died.

A bad omen for the company that would later bear his name.

great company in many respects. There was one serious problem, however, a problem that would later end up killing the company, in my opinion. So I kept declining Doug's offers.

Doug was a very good executive, but he had come up through sales. He understood sales and marketing intuitively, but he did not understand development. In a software company driven by sales and marketing, you need a very strong vice president of engineering to counter-balance the power; otherwise, you too often end up with products that do not work as well as the brochures might indicate. Icarian was funded by some of the valley's best venture capitalists, so I know that Doug got some very good advice when he hired his vice president of engineering. I also believe that the vice president he eventually hired was competent and perhaps excellent in his prior role. The problem was that those were not normal times. It was the peak of the Internet bubble.

The valley was broken; it was only a matter of time before this became evident to everyone. Down in the trenches, it was obvious a bit earlier. There were too many people who normally would have managed only small groups who were directors of whole departments, too many junior developers taking on senior-level tasks, and too many vice presidents who normally would only have been directors. There was too much money chasing too many ideas, and too many companies had huge holes in their capabilities that their senior management had no idea about.

At Icarian, the problem in engineering was that the vice president was used to managing large groups of senior and seasoned people — people who were competent in their roles and knew what they could and could not do. His previous company also had a very good reputation for recruiting excellence, so he had only had to manage those who were good at what they did. His style of management worked at his previous company.

In a startup, things are different. When work needs doing, someone will jump in and start doing that work. Sometimes, in an effort to get things done, people jump in over their heads. They commit to deadlines they cannot possibly keep. They promise features they don't know how to implement. Generally, this is done with good intent. Icarian was filled with fresh hires, new Stanford and UC Berkeley graduates, smart as hell but lacking perspective and experience. This only made the problem worse.

Being vice president of engineering in this kind of environment was not a task for someone who grew up managing seasoned competence. Icarian's vice president was incapable of managing the situation because he didn't even realize at first that there was a problem. This situation resulted from his being out of touch with the technology we used. In his previous company, that worked fine. At Icarian, given all the other variables, it was disaster.

I remember within the first week or so that I was at Icarian I saw a chart in the Quality Assurance Department (known as QA) that told me that engineering was in trouble. It was a simple chart that tracked the total number of bugs found in the software and the number of bugs fixed each week. One two-second look at that page told me that Icarian's planned software release to customers the following week was pure fantasy. The number of bugs found was increasing faster than they were being fixed, which meant that the total number of bugs in the software was climbing each week. This was a sign of software development that was out of control.

I dropped by Doug Merrit's office that same day and told him that he had a more serious problem with his current version of the software than he knew. While he and the new vice president of engineering already knew they had a problem—that was why they were looking to redesign the software and why they had sought my help with its design—they didn't have the time to wait for a new rewrite of the software. They had customers who were going to judge them on the software they already shipped. They didn't have time. They needed to start fixing their existing product, which would require a focused effort on the part of their best engineers. I felt that with my prodding, Icarian would be okay. I would work with the vice president of engineering and chief technologist to solve our common problem.

Eventually, Doug Merritt offered me a vice president–level position responsible for a new product line. I liked working at Icarian, so I accepted. Within days of this decision, however, it became clear that many within the organization were not happy with Doug's promotion of me and my conversion from a nonthreatening consultant to a vice president of a major new product. I can guess who might have felt passed over or threatened, but the bottom line is that within a few days it became clear that my promotion was a mistake. I didn't really like alienating people who I had come to know as friends, so I decided to move on and seek other consulting work.

A week or so after I left, I scheduled lunch with Doug. I wanted to tell him the unadulterated truth about his vice president of engineering. I told him that his engineering department was dysfunctional far beyond his comprehension and that if he didn't fire his vice president of engineering immediately, he was going to end up doing it in six months, but that if he waited until then, the problems with customers would be so great that they it might put the company's very survival at stake.

Doug asked me why I hadn't expressed this in such stark terms earlier. I told him that I had always envisioned myself being part of the solution, that the vice president was a good guy, but that without someone like me who understood the technology and how to manage broken projects to help him see what to do, he had no chance. In short, my leaving made firing the vice president necessary. He needed someone else in senior management who understood technology.

Doug took my advice very seriously. I heard that he even moved his office into the middle of the engineering department for a while. The problem was that Doug couldn't reconcile his sense that the vice president of engineering was competent and a smart guy with the reality that he was in over his head. Since Doug didn't have a software development background, he didn't understand the problem viscerally, as he would have if there were problems in the sales department.

About six months later, I was working at another startup, and Doug called me to meet for lunch. Over lunch he told me that he was about to fire the vice president of engineering. He asked for my help in finding a new one and with the transition because I knew most of the key players within Icarian. Things had turned out much as I predicted. The new customers were not happy. The product still didn't work as it was supposed to. Icarian was in trouble.

I was a bit surprised at the financial condition of the company when I returned. Not eight or nine months earlier, Icarian had raised over $150 million in additional funding from some of the valley's most seasoned venture capitalists, including Kleiner, Perkins, *the biggest name* in the valley. The company must have been bleeding cash. In my estimation, the buggy product was responsible directly or indirectly for most of this drain. To make customers happy, the company needed to plant a team of five to eight engineers and project managers onsite fixing problems that came up at each customer. Each sale would result in an immediate cash drain. The company would price this additional work into each quote, but then it would end up eating the costs when the customers found out how many bugs were in the product. By my estimate, the lack of a viable product was costing them perhaps 40 to 50 percent of the entire operating budget in additional related costs.

Over the next six months, and after a series of layoffs, I helped Icarian to find a new vice president of engineering and fix its problems with the product. But by the time the customers were happy, the bloom was off the Internet rose. Time had passed Icarian by. They ended up with further layoffs and eventually sold out to another company. Like its namesake Icarus, Icarian flew a little too close to the sun and crashed when its wings could no longer keep it floating.

The time to fire the vice president of engineering was six months earlier. Had this been done, perhaps Icarian's fate would have turned out differently.

But that's the trouble with startups. One mistake can kill you. Delaying or putting off needed action by even a few weeks or months can spell the difference between great success and great failure. To keep the dangers of risk at bay, you must always *act in time*.

thirteen

WHEN WRONG IS RIGHT

Do the right thing. It will gratify some people and astonish the rest.
— Mark Twain

The other day I was watching a clip of Bill O'Reilly interviewing Barack Obama shortly after the 2008 Democratic and Republican conventions.[1] O'Reilly was talking about the U.S. troop surge in Iraq and trying to get Obama to admit that he had been wrong for being against the troop surge. O'Reilly's premise was this:

1. Obama was against the surge in troops.

2. The level of violence in Iraq had diminished after the surge.

Therefore,

3. Obama was wrong in being against the surge.

Whether you agree with his political perspective or not, in this exchange, Bill O'Reilly exhibited a common cognitive flaw known as *outcome bias.* Outcome bias is the tendency of human beings to judge a decision based on *how it turns out,* its outcome, rather than on the *quality of the decision itself.* People who display the outcome bias think they made a good decision when things turn out well and a bad decision when things

[1] *The O'Reilly Factor,* FOX News Network, September 4, 2008

turn out poorly. From my experience, most people exhibit this tendency. They make a financial decision, and if it turns out well, they think they made a good decision; likewise, if it turns out poorly, they think it was a bad decision. The problem is that sometimes bad decisions can turn out well; other times good decisions can turn out poorly.

From O'Reilly's perspective, Obama was wrong because the troop surge turned out well. O'Reilly here displays outcome bias. Perhaps other factors were responsible for the progress made in reducing violence. Perhaps Obama's plan would have resulted in equal or better results. In order to evaluate decisions properly in retrospect, you need to consider the decision itself without considering the outcome. This is often easier than it sounds.

Isolating Bad Decisions from Bad Outcomes

There is a lot more luck and random chance involved in most outcomes than people like to admit, especially successful people. Successful people like to think that it is their own intelligence and decision-making prowess that has led to their success. Sometimes this is true, but many times success is due to sheer luck or being in the right place at the right time. Many of the millionaires made in the Internet bubble were just plain lucky.

Take Doug Merritt at Icarian. Doug was unlucky in his hire for vice president of engineering. Icarian crashed and burned. Had Doug chosen a different vice president of engineering, one who was better suited to the problems there, Icarian might well be the industry leader today.

Let's examine Doug's decision to hire the vice president of engineering he eventually ended up having to fire. Since Doug didn't have an engineering background, he was essentially taking his best guess.

The person he hired had been good in his previous senior position. He was smart. He was a seasoned executive with a proven track record. He was interviewed by board members and passed that test.

Doug also got sound advice from smart engineering people when he made the decision. I know because I met many of them later. Finally, Doug made sure that his new vice president of engineering displayed all those qualities that he knew were lacking in the previous manager.

When viewed from Doug's perspective at the time he made the decision, given what he knew and the advice he was given, I think he made a good decision. It turned out badly because of what he didn't know and what he could not realistically be expected to know given his background. If you fall prey to the outcome bias, you might think differently than I do about this, but you'd be wrong.

Doug made a good decision in his hire. His mistake was in not realizing that sometimes the best decisions turn out poorly, and sometimes you need to course correct quickly when you have done nothing wrong at all. Random chance, factors beyond your control, what you didn't know, competitors that come out of nowhere—all these factors can turn a good decision into a poor outcome.

Learning the Right Lessons

It is important to learn from the past, but if you don't understand the seventh rule for mastering risk, you may end up learning the wrong things as you make mistakes. The seventh rule for mastering risk is to focus on decisions, not outcomes, to avoid outcome bias. Evaluating decisions in retrospect is hard for many to do because it requires that you forget how things turned out in the end. It requires that you try to mentally reconstruct the decision *at the time it was made.*

A good decision is one that you would make again given exactly the same circumstances, skills, and knowledge. Sometimes through the process of making good decisions you acquire new skills and knowledge that in retrospect would cause you to make another decision. Those new skills and that new information will help with future decisions, but they were not in your possession before the decision, so it is not fair to evaluate yourself as if they were. Don't beat yourself up over what you didn't know or couldn't know then. Learn from the past, but don't dwell on it. Now that you know more and have more skills, you can do better in the future.

If you made a genuinely bad decision, it is good to acknowledge it as such. Poor outcomes sometimes have a lesson to teach you. A truly bad decision always has a big lesson for you. Did you ignore signs of problems that were clear and unambiguous? Did you ignore the advice of someone more experienced in a particular area? Did you perform only a cursory examination when a thorough one was warranted?

*The hardest part of any type of investing, entrepreneurship or angel investing style you follow is **focusing on decisions not outcomes**, and the toughest one to grasp. It is a great one to include because in the angel world decisions at the beginning of the company's existence play out throughout the life of a company. Therefore, you can do the legal, structure, due diligence and investing just right, but once the money is wired, a whole new set of things OUT of your control take over.*

—Howard Lindzon

Masters of the Trade

Good traders have mastered outcome bias. They know that you can lose money making good trading decisions and that you can make money from bad trading decisions. In trading, there is an inescapable element of random unpredictability. The best traders in the world sometimes have losing trades. The worst traders in the world sometimes have winning months or even years.

In certain market conditions, it is easy to make money. Almost anyone who tries can make money. Perhaps the best example from recent memory is the Internet bubble stock market of 1997–2000. If you bought tech stocks during those years, you made money. It was as simple as that.

The worst kind of traders are those who put their own capital and that of their investors at risk because they take foolish risks or ones that resemble a gambler's hunches. My first book, *Way of the Turtle*, describes in great detail how one can make money trading and the differences between a good trader and a bad trader. I will repeat the main lessons here:

Trade with an edge. Find a trading strategy that will produce positive returns over the long run.

Manage risk. Control risk so that you can continue to trade, or you may not be around for the long run, and then you won't see those positive returns.

Be consistent. Execute your plan consistently to achieve the returns.

Keep it simple. A simple plan or idea will hold up better over time than a more complex one.

These are the lessons I learned as a Turtle. They make it easy to determine what makes a good decision and what makes a bad decision when trading. For example, if you make a trade without any strategy, that is a bad trade; if you don't control risk, that is a bad trade; if you don't trade consistent with your own style, that is a bad trade; and if you add too much complexity, that is trading poorly.

Notice how these assessments do not relate to whether or not the trade made any money. Good trades are trades that are done according to the preceding principles. Some of them will lose money.

With many profitable trading strategies, most of the trades will be losing trades. But a few big winning trades can make up for all the losses. For example, if you lose, on average, $500 on 9 trades and make $10,000 on the tenth trade, the total losses on the 9 trades will be $4,500, and the net result of all 10 trades will be a gain of $5,500. Now suppose that the 9 losses came in a row; if you were judging your trading on the basis of outcomes, you would think that you were a terrible trader. You might even conclude that you couldn't make any money and quit. Or you might start to question your strategy and start to deviate.

At one time, a year or so after the original Turtles' confidentiality agreement with Richard Dennis had ended, I started telling a few of my friends the specific trading strategy I used as a Turtle to make money. I gave them all the information they needed to make trades exactly as I had. I then checked in with them over the next several weeks to make sure that they were trading correctly. I did this only a few times because inevitably my friends would end up losing money.

They ended up falling victim to the outcome bias. They judged the method based on the outcome they had seen. So they would make six or seven trades in a row and lose money on every single one. Then, since they knew I made money trading the method, they didn't stop completely, but they started to change it—to take certain trades that they "liked" and to not take ones that didn't "seem right." They inevitably picked the wrong trades to skip. The end result was that they lost money on these trades. In *Way of the Turtle,* I go into greater detail about this bias as it relates to trading. In this chapter I want to talk about it in more general terms. I find that this more general knowledge of the bias outside trading specifically also helps traders to understand the bias in their trading. In the rest of this chapter I will consider the outcome bias in other domains.

The Doctors of Outcome Bias

The decisions made by emergency room doctors are perhaps the best example of how one should handle the evaluation of decisions made under uncertainty. If an ER doctor evaluated her decisions on the basis of outcomes, then it would lead to bad medicine.

Using my example from Chapter 5, if a particular surgery has a 10 percent mortality rate, meaning that 10 percent of the patients who have the surgery done die soon after, this is risky surgery. Normally, this surgery would not be considered for a patient with a less than life-threatening condition.

However, if a patient has an injury that will kill the patient 60 percent of the time without that surgery, then the correct action is to have the surgery performed because the patient will be six times more likely to live with it than without it. If an ER doctor orders the surgery, and it is performed without error, the patient still may die. This does not change the fact that absent any new information, the decision to have the surgery was still correct.

The inherent uncertainty of diagnosis and treatment means that many times the right treatment will have a bad outcome. A good doctor knows this and will continue prescribing the best possible treatment even when a few rare examples cross her path. This is the important point. Random circumstance often will result in the right treatment having a bad outcome. A good doctor will stay mindful of the actual risks involved no matter what the particular outcomes he or she has personally seen.

This is the reason that medical research is so important. It gives doctors the ability to see the broader picture. It gives them a sound statistical basis for making decisions. It is the source of the information that says that a particular operation will have a certain outcome X percent of the time and another outcome Y percent of the time. A doctor generally does not have to guess. If he has been following the latest proceedings of his profession, he will know the current outcomes for typical injuries and their respective treatments.

Nonetheless, much like trades for the trader, any given treatment may go worse than usual or better than usual. A good ER doctor knows this and tries hard not to let the relatively few examples of outcomes

---

The market does what the market does. Prospective focus on subjective decisions brings responsibility for engaging the correct constellation of responses to bear upon a particular stimulus. While [keeping in mind the] range of outcomes is prospectively useful in establishing the constellation of responses, actual outcomes are beyond a physician's and trader's control. Making active, accurate, flexible forward looking decisions is one of the markers for excellent traders and excellent ER doctors.

—**Bruce Tizes, M.D.**

he might have seen in his own career affect his view of the proper treatments. A good doctor knows that people are prone to exhibit two other cognitive biases, or errors in logic, that can make the human tendency toward outcome bias even harder to overcome.

The first, known as *recency bias*, is the tendency to weigh the most recent data more heavily in our decisions than less recent data. You remember the most recent past and give any occurrences in the recent past greater weight than occurrences that happened *before* the recent past. For traders, this means that a trade made last week will weigh more heavily than a trade made last month or last year, so a few months of losses can cause them to doubt their decision-making process more readily because those recent losses hurt more. The same can happen to doctors. If a doctor knows that a certain procedure carries a particular risk of a bad outcome, even when she knows she performed the procedure correctly, she may start to doubt herself after a series of bad outcomes in succession.

This problem of self-doubt can be exacerbated by the second bias, known as *belief in the law of small numbers*. This is the tendency to place too much significance on a relatively small number of events within a larger context. The term is taken from the statistical law of large numbers. This is a valid statistical concept that says that a large enough sample taken from a much larger population closely resembles the population from which it was drawn. This idea forms the basis of all quality-control statistical sampling and polling of individual preferences. The sample of 500 people can provide good estimations of interest or perspective for a population of 200 million people if the sample is constructed properly.

The sample size must be large enough, however. A very small number of samples does not tell you very much about the underlying population. A poll of six people won't tell you much about the likely winner in a political race.

For this reason, my pet name for belief in the law of small numbers is the *ESPN bias*. This is a bias that shows up in sports quite often. There, you might see something like Rodriquez is batting 0.666 against Johnson on Wednesday afternoon games. What they leave out is that Rodriquez had precisely six at bats and got hits four times in these three games. With so few games and so few at-bats, you really can't draw any conclusions whatsoever.

The combination of these two biases can be devastating to one's confidence in the face of a series of adverse outcomes. They can cause you to doubt your strategy or approach when there is nothing wrong with either one. This can cause you to implement or follow a worse strategy at precisely the worst time.

Unbiasing

Fighting outcome bias requires a significant internal fortitude — confidence that no matter what the outcome, your decision is correct. In the face of uncertainty, this can be difficult. Fortunately, there are two different strategies for acquiring this fortitude that are quite effective. One strategy works under conditions of change and *chaotic uncertainty*, and one works under conditions of *informational uncertainty*.

For *chaotic uncertainty*, such as that found in trading and ER medicine, research can provide a statistical basis for understanding the likely outcomes given a range of choices. This statistical knowledge of the behavior characteristics of the future provides a firm foundation for decisions made under chaotic uncertainty. You may not know that a particular trade will work out, but it helps when you know that 18 percent of the trades were profitable when a particular strategy was tested using historical pricing data from the last 25 years. You may not know that a particular emergency heart massage is going to work when a patient's heart has stopped beating, but you do know that it will work often enough to warrant an attempt for a short while when you know that many studies have indicated that this procedure is effective when done soon after the heart stops beating and before the brain cells have died because of lack of oxygen.

For *informational uncertainty*, such as that found more often in business, you don't have quite the hard data that you do with trading and medicine. There are too many variables. So, here, the important strategy is to have a well-understood plan outlined ahead of time and a monitoring system in place that ties into that plan so that you know what you are going to do when the future unfolds under differing scenarios. The key idea is that this plan is developed ahead of time and kept up-to-date as reality unfolds. There always should be plans for what will happen if assumptions about the future are incorrect. There should be monitoring systems put in place to ensure that assumptions remain valid as time goes on.

If these conditions are met, then the evaluation of decisions is relatively easy. Did you make the best decision at the time? Did you monitor reality actively? Did you change course when warranted?

By preparing yourself adequately for the future, you can avoid outcome bias because your focus will be on the present reality and what it tells you rather than on the past and the decisions you have made that were "wrong." In uncertain conditions, it is far more important that you pay attention to what is currently actually happening than that you are able to predict what will happen far into the future.

Remember, a path that seemed at first to be wrong is right if reality unfolds differently than you expect.

In Part One, I explained each of the seven rules for mastering risk in detail. In Part Two, I offer a series of three essays with some practical implications for these rules. As you read the next part, keep in mind the key point that the implementation of the seven rules allows for a *much greater level of flexibility and safety in times of uncertainty.*

Part Two

PRACTICAL IMPLICATIONS OF THE SEVEN RULES

fourteen

READING, WRITING, AND CONFORMITY

And what is a good citizen? Simply one who never says, does, or thinks anything that is unusual. Schools are maintained in order to bring this uniformity up to the highest possible point. A school is a hopper into which children are heaved while they are still young and tender; therein they are pressed into certain standard shapes and covered from head to heels with official rubber-stamps.
—Henry Louis (H. L.) Mencken

To learn, you need to make mistakes. You need to do the wrong thing at times. You need to be willing to fail.

Kids know this instinctively. They learn to walk by falling down a lot. They learn to speak by saying things incorrectly for a few years. They learn about heat by burning themselves once or twice. They learn to listen to their parents by failing to do so a few times and noticing the consequences. They also learn by not having adults around monitoring them all the time.

Kids learn what they like and who they are by experimenting. As a society, we fail our children if we make our schools an environment where only one way is right. Children need room to be individuals and to learn that risk and failure are acceptable.

Our schools largely fail to help kids develop by experimenting and failing. Instead they serve to conform them and make them shun risk.

At the same time, our society faces ever accelerating change and uncertainty as we move from a world dominated by a few large post-colonial powers to a world of many countries cooperating and trading in a huge international web. We face competition from countries where children who are better educated grow up to be workers willing to work for far less than their American counterparts. We face competition from countries where children grow up in an environment where risk-taking, experimentation, and entrepreneurial spirit are stronger than here in the United States.

Further, our world faces several potentially devastating problems that if not addressed in the next decade or so could well mean the death and suffering of hundreds of millions of people. Global warming has already overwhelmed the most pessimistic forecasts of polar ice melt and climate change. Many of the world's most populous cities will be under water in a few decades if the pace continues. Peak oil will result in increasing tension between those with a steady supply of oil—or the means to purchase one—and those who do not. Food and clean water shortages will overwhelm the governments of developing nations and continue to destabilize entire regions.

If we don't work together to develop solutions to our largest problems then we will likely face these crises. Solutions will require a new burst of innovation in ecological technologies. Developing these innovations requires that we experiment and run risks. Incremental improvements may not be enough.

The United States has the world's largest economy and has consistently led in technology and innovation. Yet the largest portion of our pure science research and development is focused on small incremental improvements. Under normal circumstances this might not be a problem. With our current crises, we may need more. We should plan for this.

To do this, we need to start with our education system and our children.

.... 🐢 ....

As I have wandered through life, certain themes keep coming back again and again, especially my own sense that my perspective on risk is extremely uncommon, that others look at risk very differently than I do. While writing this book, I thought long and hard about what it was that allowed me to develop my views and at the same time maintain an internal sense of what is important. I believe that much of this difference stems from the way I grew up.

I grew up learning from outside adventures with friends in the forests and fields behind my house. My father always made sure that we lived next to open space. Even when we lived in the suburbs of Chicago, we lived next to a 40-acre forest preserve that was owned by the county. My father did this because he thought a house located next to open land would maintain better value as an investment. As a side benefit, this investment decision provided my brother, my sister, and me with the opportunity to play freely, unsupervised, on most afternoons. In the outdoors, I grew up taking risks and sometimes failing.

The independent and self-reliant spirit we developed playing in our own little wilderness was a strong bulwark against the oppressive squeeze toward conformity, docile acceptance, and standardization that is our modern school system. For many people, schools simply beat them into shunning risk and difference.

Modern Schools

The modern school system, where everyone is expected to be a high school graduate, has not been around as long as many of you might think. Before World War I, most adults in the United States did not have a high school education. They worked on farms or in factories. A high-school education was reserved for those who would go on to attend the relatively few colleges and universities. It was reserved for the children of the elite.

In the early 1930s, President Franklin D. Roosevelt knew that an education system that had worked well during the era of a mostly agrarian United States was not providing for the industrial age and the age of modern management. So a large initiative was started to provide for the public schooling of all children through the twelfth grade. It was thought that high school would be better training for jobs in the large companies just then starting to dominate the U.S. economy. The new program was also designed to keep teenagers from competing economically with grown men during the depths of the Great Depression.

So our current education system was conceived of as a place for the production of workers who would fit within a larger system of industry. It was conceived of as a place where *"children are heaved while they are still young and tender; therein they are pressed into certain standard shapes."* It was not conceived of as a place where one would develop specific independent talents and aptitudes. It was not conceived of as a place where it was okay to take risks.

Given our current environment and circumstances, it is time we reconceived our school system to confront the modern reality where change and uncertainty reign. Our industry is no longer dominated by industrial behemoths. It is time we adapted our education system to match our new needs.

School is not a place that teaches us to question and probe. In schools we are taught implicitly and often explicitly that authority is always correct and absolute. This perspective is incorrect, even dangerous.

From my experience, schools and the teachers in them do not like their authority questioned. They are even organized with a perspective much like factories. Put some money and some students in one end, and after 12 years, you are supposed to get educated adults out the other end. This factory approach does not work. I have seen good and great schools, but they all suffer from a tendency to reward conformity and to punish anyone who questions or does not conform to their ideal.

School was pretty easy for me. But even at my high school, which was one of the top schools in Massachusetts, it was mostly rote memorization that didn't challenge. We were not taught the causes and effects of history, but the events and dates. We were not taught to think, but to know facts rather than principles. We were not alone in this. I later learned that schools everywhere taught knowledge but not understanding. Many teachers could tell you the whats, but very few could tell you the whys.

The Trouble with Universities

This may sound a little silly, but my primary goal in attending college was to figure out exactly how transistors worked. I remember the sophomore-year electrical engineering lecture where our professor first explained transistors at the molecular level. It was a pivotal point in my education.

I had learned about atoms and molecules and electronics in junior high school. I knew how transistors could be assembled into logic circuits to build computers. I also knew how computer programming worked, but the missing link was that I didn't understand how transistors actually worked at the molecular level. They were a mystery. So, once my professor connected them together and filled the gap by explaining how transistors worked at the molecular level, I felt like my mission at Worcester Polytechnic Institute (WPI) was done. From that point forward, trading and programming held greater interest, and WPI could teach me nothing there.

I tried a programming course at WPI but soon found that I was already doing more advanced work for George Arndt at Harvard Investment Service than the most advanced computing classes at WPI at the time. I also found that the Apple IIe computers we used were more powerful than the tiny fraction of a computer that WPI allocated to each student in the programming lab. From my perspective, there was not much point in staying at WPI, so I convinced my father that in the fall of 1983 I would try to make money trading using the methods I had been taught by my mentor, Rotchie Barker. The rest of the story can be found in my book, *Way of the Turtle*.

So I left before I graduated. I remain a college dropout.

But I have hired many college-educated people, including many with advanced degrees from Ivy League schools, and find that, in general, the higher the education level, the lower the appetite for risk. Since I first started to notice this phenomenon, I have learned quite a bit more about what it takes to earn an advanced degree, especially a Ph.D. And a Ph.D. degree is all but required if you want to do any research in science and technology in the United States. You cannot get a grant or a position at a university doing research without a Ph.D. Even private companies will not hire you for research without a Ph.D.

In a science Ph.D. program, one is supposed to add to the general knowledge in some way. As a practical matter, this means finding an academic sponsor who is already a professor (with a Ph.D.) and part of the tenured faculty and getting him or her to sponsor your research as a valid effort. This entire process weeds out those who like to take risks. A professor is unlikely to sponsor a student who wants to run experiments that disprove the professor's entire outlook.

Consider what Peter Fiske, author of *Put Your Science to Work: The Take-Charge Career Guide for Scientists*, says in a July 24, 1998, career advice column for *Science* magazine:

Furthermore, grad school can reinforce behavior that is detrimental to success, either in science or beyond. One example (that I have learned the hard way) is: risk aversion. . . .

Risk aversion is more than just the tendency to avoid risk; it is the inability to weigh risk and reward and a failure to recognize when prudent risk taking is needed. Part of the source of risk aversion in scientists may be that the career of science can be very attractive to risk-averse people! From a college grad's perspective, a science career can seem a very secure pathway—hard work seems to be rewarded with tenure and security. Once in grad school, many students find that the financially stressed, competitive world of research science actually promotes intellectual conservatism and risk aversion. Research groups make safe, incremental research steps because that is the only way to get funding. Few PIs [principal investigators, the lead contact for a grant] can get grants nowadays for proposing a wacky idea outside their subdiscipline. And students learn this lesson fully. Have you ever seen someone try a daring new project for their thesis, fail to make it work, and still get a Ph.D.?

In my experience, this holds true. It is the rare Ph.D. scientist who can overcome risk aversion to the extent required to be an effective member of a startup. Most simply cannot tolerate the risks associated with that kind of venture. This effectively means that the vast majority of people doing basic science research in the United States are those who are risk averse.

Bottom-Up Research

We U.S. citizens spend a lot of money on basic scientific research. Our current approach provides an excellent mechanism for incremental improvement, taking the state of the art just a little bit further over time.

It does not provide very well for revolutionary improvements, the kind we may soon require to avert ecological and sociological disaster as we fill the earth with people who will not have enough energy, food, or water. So it benefits us all to improve our search for the answers to some of the questions that we need resolved.

For example, the incremental progress shown for alternative-energy technologies may not be enough. Indeed, it seems unlikely that these technologies will be sufficient to keep global warming at bay. In many instances, the world's developing economies simply lack the money or infrastructure for these more expensive and complex alternatives. In other instances, governments lack the political will sufficient to accept the tradeoffs required by these alternatives.

So how do we create workable change? How do we increase the chances our research will yield the kind of revolutionary advances that might make fusion power viable, for instance? We need to open our research to include ideas outside the mainstream. To do this we need to start at the source of the problem, funding.

The funding mechanism for most U.S. scientific research is through research funding grants. Ph.D. scientists generally propose specific projects that are reviewed by the agencies for potential benefit. The review panels are generally other Ph.D. scientists familiar with the area of investigation. They base their evaluations on criteria that are similar to the following list:

- *Scientific merit of the project*
- *Appropriateness of the approach*
- *Competency of applicant's personnel*
- *Adequacy of applicant's resources*
- *Reasonableness of the budget*

(Summarized from information on the Department of Energy's Web site.)

Note that the first two criteria will tend to filter out ideas that are "wild" or different from the established scientific orthodoxy. If a panel of scientists is deciding whether or not to fund a grant for scientific research, it will not choose to fund an idea that the panelists don't think has a chance of working. It will not find an approach "appropriate" if the panelists do not think it will work either.

Likewise, the panelists will tend to judge the competency of personnel on the traditional scientific merits: the school they attended, the other scientists they have worked with, and the scientific papers they have published, among other things. But the process of peer review for scientific papers is itself one that stifles rogue ideas. So the scientists who get published are the ones who conform to accepted scientific orthodoxy. This means that the grant panelists will find only those who have accepted this orthodoxy to be competent researchers.

Yet it is often the renegade thinkers who come up with the major breakthroughs. Many leading scientists did not accept Albert Einstein's theory of relativity until it could be experimentally proven. Einstein could not find work in academia, he had to work as a patent clerk because he was too much of a renegade. It is likely that most grant approval panels would not have found Thomas Edison to be a competent scientific investigator either.

So one way we can greatly increase the possibility of our science and technology research making a breakthrough rather than just incremental improvement is by partially decentralizing and democratizing the research funding process. We could do this is by turning the funding process upside down.

Right now, small panels decide what gets funded, and a large group of scientists does the actual research. Instead, we could divide up a portion of the budget and allow individual research scientists and engineers a say in how the money gets spent. For example, the budget could be divided into salary and laboratory costs and each research scientist or engineer might be allocated a salary of $100,000 and a lab budget of $100,000 per year.

Each scientist then could be allocated a vote in how to spend his or her portion of the research budget. An individual scientist or engineer could choose to work on a small project by herself, or she could join up with other scientists to work on larger problems. Junior scientists or lab assistants could choose to work for more senior scientists, and the junior scientist's lab budget would be allocated to the more senior scientist. These allocations could be readjusted each year to allow research to quickly adapt as new discoveries are made.

This approach might strike some as crazy. It isn't. It is the approach that nature takes during times of change: Try many things, kill bad ideas quickly, nourish good ideas, and use them as the basis for other new ideas. This is the approach that our scientists and engineers used during the early days of the *Apollo* project, and it is the approach used by the best engineering organizations today, like Google. Let the individual scientists and engineers have some say in what they work on. These individuals are smart enough to know what is important, what work needs to be done, and where they can individually add value.

If we implement an approach like this for at least a portion of our science and technology research then we can expect to attract a more diverse group of students to science programs at our universities. The individualists and iconoclasts that shun the large bureaucracies of academic research might be attracted to science if they could explore outside the bounds of the mainstream and without the requirements for paperwork and reporting associated with today's grant-based scientific research.

But first we must make sure that these types of individuals are attracted to science and technology careers in the first place. To do this, we need to make sure they are not first discouraged by an education system that does not promote risk-taking and individuality. We must go back to how we teach science and mathematics in our primary and secondary school systems.

Education is important; too important for us to tolerate the current conditions. We cannot have a system that weeds out and discourages the risk-takers and adventurers. We cannot expect to innovate our way out of our current problems if we do not support a spirit of experimentation and discovery by failure in our education.

We need to provide room for our children to experiment and fail, to learn by trying. Our current education system does not serve this need.

We as a society cannot expect that a system that tries to turn out standard-shaped and "educated" adults is going to work very well when the very fabric of our society is changing as fast as it is. This process of uniformity and conformity building hampers societal adaptability. Organizations that are adaptive and more organic in nature always win out over organizations that are more highly specialized. Individuals who are more individually adaptive will have greater success than those who are only successful in a highly specific set of circumstances.

There is one thing of which we can be certain: The future will bring something unexpected. So we should stop educating our children as if we know exactly what they will need 10 to 20 years down the road. We don't.

fifteen

RISKING TOGETHER

It's not because things are difficult that we dare not venture.
It's because we dare not venture that they are difficult.
—Lucius Annaeus Seneca

As individuals, we often don't handle uncertainty and risk very well. As groups, we mostly fail utterly.

Most people are naturally risk-averse. Through socialization, groups magnify this aversion. A bureaucracy is the strongest magnifier.

In a bureaucracy, the goal is to maintain a position or climb higher. In no event does an employee in a bureaucracy want to do anything that might jeopardize his or her continued ability to maintain position or climb the ladder of power. This has the practical effect of filtering risk-takers out of the promotion chain. Further, since bureaucracies are characterized by rules and procedures, any attempts to change the way of doing things will meet resistance by those who will see a push for change as a push for power and a potential assault on their position within the hierarchy.

Corporate hierarchies are risk-averse, but government bureaucracies are even more risk-averse. This leads to significant waste because, unlike corporate bureaucracies, government bureaucracies tend not to go away or shrink. They tend to grow even when they are inefficient and do not meet their original intent. If a corporation fails to be efficient, it will end up in bankruptcy because of competition with companies that are more efficient. Government bureaucracies, in contrast, tend to have mandated monopolies. They are generally granted funding each year whether they have fulfilled their purpose or not. Each person in the hierarchy tries to justify greater and greater budgets each year whether they have been effective or not. The net result is that we have funding that does not correlate with our current problems and priorities. These generalizations are true at the city, county, state, and federal levels.

In this chapter I will first consider the ways that corporations and nongovernment organizations (NGOs) can implement the seven rules for mastering risk to manage uncertainty more effectively. Second, I will consider some ways that governments and quasi-governmental organizations can do much the same. Before I do, I need to outline some of the problems with a hierarchical command and control structure, the most common organizational structure for corporations and governments.

Truth Distortion

As covered previously several times, there can be no effective management of uncertainty without a firm grasp of reality. One cannot make decisions under uncertainty without a good sense of the current status. Hierarchies cloud the truth because it is in the best interest of each manager to characterize reality in the most favorable terms possible. This tendency is multiplied with each level in the hierarchy. The people at the top know far less about what is actually going on than do those at the bottom. Anyone who works for a large company knows that this is true. This inability to perceive reality while looking down through the lens of a hierarchy impedes both corporations and governments from being able to take risks effectively.

The problem is that levels in hierarchies multiply the effect known colloquially as "the fox watching the henhouse." Each manager is responsible both for managing her respective area and for reporting progress and status for that area. There is generally no independent guide to judge the veracity of any reporting outside of finance. The truth is difficult to determine from the top looking down through this lens of distortion.

For this reason, the most important factor in a company's ability to operate under uncertainty is whether or not they exhibit culture of truth. The best-run companies have a culture where telling the truth is encouraged even when that truth is difficult. This is very hard to do in a medium-sized company. It is almost impossible to do in a large company.

Rigidity

The second major problem with bureaucracies is their inflexibility. The second rule for mastering risk is to remain flexible. Bureaucracies are the very antithesis of a flexible organization. Rules, procedures, and policies define their means of operation. Government is generally even worse. Combine rigidity with a lack of truth and you have a recipe for the waste of enormous sums of money. Unfortunately, it is a recipe that is commonly followed.

Rules and procedures are often implemented in an attempt to compensate for a lack of trust between upper- and lower-level management. One example of a set of rules of this type might be rigid hiring procedures. For example, in order to hire a new employee in a bureaucratic company, a first-level manager might have to gain the approval of three or four levels of management several times. To start the process, a hiring manager would first need a job requisition approved. This approval generally will trigger a process in human resources to start recruiting. Then another approval would be needed for the actual compensation package for the particular person who will be hired. These approvals sometimes can take days or weeks at each level, thereby slowing the hiring process by months.

Rigid rules and procedures are also used to compensate for lack of clear leadership. Organizations that trust their people and give clear direction do not need rigid rules, even if they are large organizations. The vast majority of large- and medium-sized organizations do not exhibit these two critical traits. They replace trust with controls and approval processes. They replace clarity of direction with specifications and formal procedures. This can prove fatal when the organization needs to change because it can take months or years to change a set of rules and procedures. A good leader can change the strategic direction of a large organization very quickly, in days or weeks.

It takes years to change the direction of a bureaucracy. This can prove disastrous when the organization has serious responsibilities that require quicker action. It can result in tens or even hundreds of billions of dollars of waste when a bureaucracy grows larger and does not meet its objectives because of inflexibility.

Restructuring the Corporation

So the question remains: What can be done to increase the flexibility of corporations and to heighten their ability to implement the seven rules for mastering risk? First, I will consider some ways that companies can clear up truth distortion. Second, I will examine ways that companies can become more flexible.

Tackling the problem of truth distortion is the first step any corporation must undertake to be able to respond well. Large corporations that do not have an ongoing culture of looking squarely at reality can take some significant steps to removing truth distortion by reexamining their own internal check-and-balance systems. Corporate financial reporting systems, in general, show an adequate accounting of the truth of financial expenditures, but they are only a partial step.

In order to arrive at a solution to the problem, we should consider again the major factor that stifles truth telling in an organization—the truth distortion at each step in the hierarchy. Employees and managers are often afraid of describing reality as they see it when they believe it will harm their prospects for promotion and may even get them fired. To overcome this requires a parallel organization headed by a leader who reports directly to the board of directors, charged with the sole task of adequately reporting status and the current realities.

Such an organization would have as its charter only the accurate dissemination of status and information—financial status, project status, marketing status, everything to do with reality and the corporation's position vis-à-vis that reality. The employment status of everyone in this organization would not be affected by normal management, so each of these employees would be secure, knowing that their employment depended on accurately reporting information without hierarchical stifling.

The creation of a parallel organization charged with tracking reality is only a partial step as well. Another significant factor that hampers accurate status-taking is the fear of retribution by management. Employees are afraid that if they tell a story different from the one their boss is telling, they will be fired or passed up for promotion in the future. In many companies, this perspective is correct. Employees do pay a price for contradicting their bosses, even when they are telling the truth in the contradiction. This phenomenon is bad for the company.

I don't know a single CEO or senior executive who wants to be misinformed about bad news. In general, they all know that it is better to get bad news as soon as possible, while there is still time to do something about it.

In the last 20 or 30 years, there have been increasing signs that the traditional organizational hierarchies or pyramids don't work very well. Project-oriented companies have experimented with other styles, including what is known as a *matrix organization*. In a matrix organization, each employee has two bosses. One is a domain expert, and one is a manager specific to a particular project on which the employee is currently working. The idea of a matrix approach is that it increases the flexibility of an organization because people can be reassigned to different projects and yet still maintain a continuing relationship with the boss who is an expert in their work domain. For this reason, companies with a large component of external consulting work, such as Accenture, IBM, and most of the management consulting companies, often have matrix organizations.

Here is how a matrix organization might work: Imagine that you are a technical writer assigned to a project for putting in place a new production line in a candy bar factory. Your job is to write out a manual for all the machines for each of the stations on the production line with control settings specific to your line of candy bars. In this case, you report to two different people. You report to the project manager, Mary, who is responsible for getting the entire production line up and running. She has a project team that includes you as well as millwrights, electronic process control engineers, and chemical engineers.

Since you work for a matrix organization, you also report to a more senior technical writer, Mark, who is responsible for mentoring you, helping to evaluate your work, and placing you on projects appropriate to your skills and experience as they come up.

Unfortunately, this matrix organization, while seemingly an improvement over a strict pyramid, still suffers from a major flaw—the lack of visibility into the truth. Suppose that production is delayed for several weeks because of damage to machinery caused by inaccuracies in the settings as defined in the manual. These wrong settings could be caused by bad information coming from the process control engineers who understand the machinery or from the chemical engineers who understand how to make candy bars in bulk, or it could result from inattention to detail by you, the technical writer.

It will be difficult for either of your bosses to determine who caused the problem. It will be even more difficult for the plant manager to understand the source of the problem because it will likely become a "he said/she said" issue, with each group blaming the others. So the problem won't get fixed quickly, if at all.

To solve this problem requires another rethinking of the typical corporate hierarchy, where a boss is responsible for the hiring and firing of employees. A better approach would be to have each employee have three senior contacts in the company: one human resources contact the employee would talk with for discussions about benefits and who would be responsible for hiring and firing decisions, one technical mentor who would be a senior employee who can evaluate the employee's work product and can help the employee develop, and the project manager or boss who is responsible for day-to-day work assignments.

Why is it important to separate the hiring and firing function from the domain hierarchy and the project manager? It is important because knowing the truth is the most important prerequisite to a responsive, flexible organization. If an employee is afraid of telling the truth, then you won't get the truth easily. This damages the entire organization.

As more companies move to an environment where the technical requirements for individual employees are based on more advanced training and knowledge, it becomes increasingly important to be able to hire and retain quality employees lest you lose all their training and knowledge. If a company spends months on specialized training, the turnover of an employee is a big waste of both money and time. This is why I suggest breaking the traditional "boss" role and hierarchy into three separate pieces: the career-guidance role and hierarchy, generally now called *human resources*, but I prefer Ann Rhoades's name choice of "people department." Ann coined this name when she headed the people department at Southwest Airlines; the domain-specific mentor role, taken by a more senior technologist, accountant, machinist, salesperson, etc., who, in turn, is mentored by more senior mentors; and the management role and hierarchy, taken by someone in the traditional hierarchy who is responsible for defining the work the employee is required to perform.

Employees in a company with this type of structure would be far more likely to tell the truth to their counterpart in the reality organization. Their manager would not have the power to fire them or ruin their career in the company because that would no longer be a manager's prerogative. In the new structure, employees would be encouraged by their *people* advisor and their *mentor* to tell the truth, especially when it was bad news, because that would be one of the roles of their respective hierarchy.

In an organization of this proposed type, instead of the traditional single chain of command and hierarchy, we have

> **Management.** Makes decisions about what gets done, sets priorities, defines work for employees, reports status to appropriate parties involved in ensuring accuracy, proposes new projects, and implements new projects by getting new employees assigned from the *people* department.

People. Recruits and hires employees based on suitability of employee to company, works with management to fill job openings for new projects with existing staff and new hires, assesses employee happiness and job satisfaction, and assesses employee performance from an interaction perspective; fires employees who do not prove competent or a good fit for the company's culture.

Mentoring. Makes decisions about who is capable of what tasks for projects, sets training goals and deadlines, proposes new projects to management, works with the *people* department to keep employees happy by making sure that they are doing work that challenges them sufficiently, makes sure that employees are not in over their heads without assistance, and assesses the technical quality of employees' work and reports to *people, management,* and *reality.*

In general, the creation of four hierarchies from one may seem like it would require a lot of additional people, but most companies could staff these departments using existing people without disrupting work. In most companies, departments such as auditing and quality assurance would naturally fall into the *reality* department. Most of human resources likely would fall into the *people* department. The mentors in a company generally already exist, so creating a department should be a matter of looking at each level of management and then finding the people who employees already look to for guidance; these are the natural mentors who should be taken into the *mentoring* hierarchy.

This approach greatly increases the ability of senior management to know the truth about the company's status and direction. It also makes the company much more flexible.

Restructuring Government

Governments are the most inflexible form of organization we have. With corporations, inefficiencies in a corporation's operating methods *eventually* will result in a drop in the share price with a corresponding change in management. A government organization has no such obvious measure of success or failure. Long after a government agency or department's purpose has ended, it will continue to exist, grow, and draw from the national treasury.

Government is further complicated by the interjection of the legislative function of Congress. These policymakers add another layer of inflexibility. The executive branch is constrained by what it is able to do according to laws generated by the legislative branch. The legislators also control priorities by means of budgets. Finally, they add another layer of risk aversion.

The combination of bureaucracy and the additional layer of indirection provided by Congress makes government the least-innovative, slowest, and least-productive means for working together as a group. Acknowledgment of this truth has been one of the biggest factors in the trend toward government outsourcing in recent years.

Risk with Critical Challenges

Unfortunately, there are some tasks that are simply too large for companies or groups of people to tackle by themselves. Additionally, whether because of budget constraints or because the profit motive of corporations is too short sighted, there are some areas where the government is the best actor possible.

Even so, there are certain things that the government must do that require a different approach than we have been using. These are the critical challenges that we must meet as a society: educating all our children, developing clean energy technologies, eliminating poverty, and improving our transportation infrastructure. Each of these challenges is important for different reasons, but they share one characteristic—our approaches for solving them have failed so far. Utterly.

I propose that the primary reason that we have failed is because of our approach to risk. We have created risk-averse and failure-averse bureaucracies and charged them with challenges that we do not know how to solve. Our bureaucracies look in vain for the one true, safe way to success.

Since we do not know how to solve these problems, we should run a lot of experiments. We should try many different approaches.

We should apply the same four principles that guided Alfred Sloan at General Motors during its high-growth years:

Experiment. Try many approaches rather than just one or two.

Differentiate. Try very different approaches.

Adapt. Learn from what works, and continue to change and adapt your strategy as you find success.

Organize organically. Make sure that your plans account for the fact that the future will bring something you cannot anticipate.

No Child Left Behind

How could we do this at the federal government level? We might first consider the wrong approach. The Department of Education with the No Child Left Behind Act (NCLB) serves as one good example. This act is a great example of good intention meets centralized bureaucracy.

I am not a policy wonk. I haven't spent years looking at education policy, so I don't know the ins and outs of the history of the fight between the various policy factions and the recent rise of standards-based education reform. But I do know a bit about the failure of our education system. I have talked with educators and administrators about the problem as research for the book that will follow this one. I also come from a family of educators. Five of my aunts and uncles have been teachers. One uncle has taught in ghetto schools for over 30 years. I have talked with them about the causes of our education failure.

I also helped teach an after-school reading program in a ghetto school in one of the worst public school districts in the United States, in the U.S. Virgin Islands town of Charlotte Amalie. I saw with my own eyes how eager kids were to learn. I saw how it was the adults who were failing them.

So, when I consider NCLB, I am an educated outsider. I examine it with respect to how well it is working and how well it adheres to the seven rules for mastering risk, and it fails, as pointed out earlier. I find the same problems with the Department of Education as is typical of any top-down hierarchy—good intentions and a lack of understanding of the impact of the directives on those who actually implement them. Management is out of touch with the troops.

The basic premise of the act is good: By measuring student progress, it should be possible to evaluate the effectiveness of the teachers and school systems. This is an example of standards-based education reform. NCLB does not specify a set of standards for each state—because education is the domain of the states under Article X of the U.S. Constitution—but it specifies that each state must develop its own standards and must administer reading, science, and math tests to each child roughly once per year starting in third grade through middle school and once during high school. There are plenty of proponents and opponents of the bill itself, but I don't want to cover the traditional reasons for or against the act. Instead, I want to look at why it fails the Sloan model.

No experiments. First, the act is too specific. While skirting the letter of the Constitution by leaving the specifics of the testing to the states, it mandates too much, and so much federal funding is at risk that states have no real choice but to comply. This is a problem because it *prevents states from experimenting* with approaches that might work much better. Is testing third graders a good idea? Under NCLB, we won't find out because all states must test third graders.

No differentiation. The act does not encourage differentiation. It is much easier for a state to adopt standards similar to those of other states than to adopt radically different ones.

No adaptation. The act is too constraining. States are not allowed to diverge and adapt their own programs based on success or failure. The testing itself is a given. The states can change the tests themselves or the standards, but not the idea of testing-based education and the frequency of the tests.

Inorganic organization. The top-down structure of a federal mandate is the polar opposite of an organic bottom-up structure. An organic organization would start with the teachers' and students' perspectives, not the legislators' perspective.

A Better Act

So how might we restructure a program like NCLB to make it more responsive and organic? How could we greatly increase our chances of improving the education of our children in meaningful ways? How might we apply the Sloan process in the Department of Education?

First, we need to recognize that the fundamental idea of standards-based education has its merits. It is an attempt to determine reality so that we can judge progress and compare among the various schools to determine which are doing well, which are middling, and which are doing poorly. There is a saying that you can't fix something if you don't know why it is broken. The testing in NCLB is an attempt to get some real data.

The program fails for various reasons, much like a similar program would fail in the corporate world. Truth does not rise in a hierarchy. Teachers fudge results so that they look better. In many schools, teachers teach what they think will be on the test and little else. School districts fudge results. And when that doesn't work, some states have admitted to lowering their standards so that they can show improvement when there has been no such improvement.

The Federal Role

The best way to encourage experimentation, differentiation, adaptation, and organic organization is by defining the rules at a very high level and providing support, but then getting out of the way. The federal government is meddling too specifically in state-level issues.

The feds ought to set up education like an annual contest in which the target is relative improvement—getting better each year. They themselves ought to administer the tests but do so on a random-sampling basis. This is much like the suggestion of creating a truth-seeking department within a company. Since the federal governance is separate from the state governance, federal testers have no incentive to fudge the results. So the states should be allowed to develop whatever programs and curricula they want with the knowledge that the federal government will be testing random samples of classrooms and schools across the various districts. The testing can be more frequent in areas where there are problems.

Since the classrooms would be tested randomly and with an unknown test, there will no longer be any incentive for teachers to "teach to the test." Teachers will be able to focus on teaching a more rounded curriculum. Random testing also would allow for much more subjective testing criteria because there would be much more time available for each student being tested. NCLB tests every kid. A random sample of 1 child in 20 would be more than enough to build a statistically accurate sense of a school's performance. You could cut testing resources by 75 percent and still have five times as much time available per random student tested under a random testing program.

Testing every child wastes time and money that could best be spent elsewhere. Random testing is a much more efficient use of time and money.

This type of testing also would allow for different types of testing for the younger grades. Expecting all third-grade kids to take standardized multiple-choice tests is not reasonable. Instead, the federal government should examine alternative ways of testing the kids' ability to perform at level that are not so intimidating and that don't require specific test-taking skills. For example, instead of testing a third-grade student's reading using a computer-graded standardized test, the testers could evaluate the students using methods that include verbal questions and answers.

So, in effect, the federal government would take responsibility for evaluating each state using a standard set of tests. This would make for a true apples-to-apples comparison between the states. Right now, since each state's tests are different, it is much harder to evaluate the progress of education between each state at the lower grade levels. We are forced to use the college entrance exams, which are standardized across the entire country but which typically are administered only to eleventh-grade students. This is very late in the process, a time when it is too late to correct learning deficiencies for students who would have liked to attend college.

In this proposed new role, the Department of Education would be responsible for developing statistics that allow parents to evaluate the relative performance of each state. The states, meanwhile, freed from the onus of developing and administering their own standardized tests and associated programs, could experiment more or allow each district to experiment more. The state could even take an analogous role to the federal role within the states, administering random testing of students within each of the districts to evaluate the performance of each district.

This example could be applied to almost every area of government because almost all government departments fail to experiment, differentiate, adapt, or organize organically. They fail the Sloan test. The rigid, large-scale government that worked in the 1930s and 1940s does not work today. Our government needs to keep pace with changes in the global business environment and needs to be able to react in time to avert economic and environmental crises owing to peak oil, global warming, and the growing shortage of clean water.

The monolithic top-down hierarchies that remain in government but that have been largely purged from successful business must go. In their place we should install more organic structures. Our challenge as citizens over the next several years and decades will be to adapt government to be more responsive. Our success as a country and even as a species may depend on it.

sixteen

JUMPING OUT OF
THAT PLANE

If we listened to our intellect, we'd never have a love affair.
We'd never have a friendship. We'd never go into business, because we'd
be too cynical. Well, that's nonsense. . . .You've got to jump off cliffs all
the time and build your wings on the way down.
—Annie Dillard

In this chapter I outline some specific steps that you can take to adapt your life to the seven rules of mastering risk. Looking at the chapter title, you might think my advice will always be to take on more risk.

This is true only some of the time. There are many instances when investors, especially those who are nearing retirement age, take on far too much risk because they do not understand the risks their investments encompass. In recent years it has become obvious that even professional investors have been largely unaware of the risks involved in their investments. Just consider the large number of bankruptcies and failures of hedge funds that invested in U.S. mortgage-backed securities that ended up being nearly worthless.

The Real-Life Risks

As a Turtle, I employed a technique known as *trend following*. Essentially, it was a way of looking at market data and deciding if a particular market was moving sideways, up, or down. The perspective I learned from this technique has caused me to view life and recent history through the same lens. I constantly look at the world and notice the bigger trends: what moves, what stays the same, and the things that have always stayed the same and are just now moving for the first time. These later ones are the new trends, the dangerous ones. Sometimes they are just cultural drifts; sometimes they are veritable upheavals.

In the last four or five decades, there have been several large trends that have surfaced risks that most people did not anticipate: outsourcing of factories with the resulting layoffs in the manufacturing sectors, globalization of large corporations with the resulting outsourcing of "safer" high-technology and service jobs such as IT consulting and call centers, and the complete dominance of the "big box" stores over smaller "mom and pop" stores.

Each of these trends started small but soon came to dominate in their respective industries. Each of these trends affected large numbers of people who thought they were safe and secure but later learned that the only constant in our economy is change and sometimes that change can shake the core of our assumptions about what is risky and what is not risky.

Consider those who had taken union factory jobs in the 1950s and 1960s. This was considered a safe, reliable way to provide an income for your family. In the 1970s, however, as the United States faced stiffer competition from overseas, many U.S. auto, steel, and manufacturing plants in the so-called rust-belt cities closed down, and many manufacturers faced bankruptcy. So those who may have worked 20 to 30 years at a factory were suddenly laid off and faced with unemployment, something they would have seen as impossible just 10 or 15 years earlier.

During the same time, many U.S. manufacturers moved their plants from the northern cities to the rural South, where they could find workers willing to work at one-third to one-half the rate of their northern counterparts. The workers in these new plants no doubt thought that they had found safe, reliable jobs, but many were wrong. After the passage of NAFTA it became more profitable for U.S. companies to move their higher-cost assembly plants just over the border to growing cities in Mexico, such as Tijuana, Juarez, Nuevo Laredo, and Matamoros. So many relatively new factories in the U.S. South were shut down after just 10 to 15 years of operation when it became profitable for companies to do so.

In the 1980s and 1990s, many U.S. students prepared themselves for technology jobs and middle-management jobs in larger companies. These seemed to be the jobs of the future. Companies that studied the job markets predicted huge increases in the staffing for IT and related services. Then came the Internet.

Now it was possible to hire English-speaking employees in India who were willing to work for one-sixth to one-eighth the salary. Employers often found that the quality of the work performed in India was better than the work done in the United States.

The real catalyst to change came during the years running up to 2000, when the code for many older computer systems needed to be updated to reflect the upcoming requirement of expressing years in four digits instead of the two digits that had worked for 40 years. This was known as the Y2K *problem*. The massive scale of the changes required caused many companies to outsource significant portions of their work to India, setting in motion the beginning of true globalization in the IT business.

After the Indian Y2K work turned out well for many companies, they started to look for other ways to save money by outsourcing U.S. jobs at lower wages. Soon call-center workers in the Midwest found their jobs replaced by those in Bangalore, Hyderabad, Mumbai, or Chandigarh. This meant that the relatively new call-center businesses established in the rural Midwest were at risk.

Each of these trends caused upheavals that exposed the risks inherent in our modern global world. Change is the only constant.

Apocalypse on the Street

As I write this chapter, Wall Street is in tatters. In just the last few weeks, Lehman Brothers, one of the few remaining investment banks, has declared bankruptcy, and Merrill Lynch has sold itself to Bank of America to avoid the same fate. AIG, the world's largest insurance company, sold a majority interest to the U.S. government. Fannie Mae and Freddie Mac, the largest holders of U.S. mortgages, have been nationalized. The U.S. stock market has seen the largest single-day drop in stock price in its history, and there were failures of two more banks—Washington Mutual and Wachovia—just this week. And the end is still not near.

The full impact of the intermingled obligations of the larger banks and insurance companies with the complicated and very highly leveraged derivatives they sold and bought from each other likely will not be known for years, if not decades.

The chaos brings two problems to the fore. First, you cannot be sure that your assumptions about what is risky and what is safe are correct. Second, you cannot rely on the so-called ratings companies such as Moody's and S&P to define the risk level of an investment. For the individual or family investing for retirement or college, the future remains even more unpredictable.

There is no longer any "safe" strategy. You can't count on anything anymore. Even state and municipal government workers are finding their positions cut as real-estate values drop, causing a corresponding drop in the property-tax revenues that pay for their jobs.

Today's world is a bit like jumping out of a plane. You may be terrified while you are in the plane, but once you are outside, your mind starts to focus on something else. You are moving toward the ground really fast. Not making a decision is no longer an option. You have to *do something*—and quickly.

When the world is moving fast and change accelerates, not making decisions or making the traditional conservative ones is no longer a safe option. You need to start applying the seven rules for mastering risk in your personal lives whether you want to or not. Not only that, but if there are no truly "safe" options, you might as well start having some fun in your careers.

For the individual as an employee or investor, the level of uncertainty surrounding today's business and social environments is higher than ever. In fact, this is a time of accelerating uncertainty. What should the individual do to deal with this greatly increased risk? In the next section I will consider some practical steps that you can take to manage your life in today's crazy times. In particular, I will explore the three rules that individuals seem to have the hardest time with: overcoming fear, remaining flexible, and focusing on outcomes.

Overcome Fear

Many people let others make their decisions because they are afraid of making the "wrong" decisions. They defer their career choices to their parents or their counselors. They defer their investment decisions to the "expert" asset manager, who simply may be a salesperson at the bank who happened to talk them into a particular deal.

Don't defer major decisions to others. They may not be as competent as you think they are. In my experience, 95 percent of the "professional" people in the investment business have no idea what they are doing. They are guessing at best and trying to predict an unpredictable future at worst. Don't put your future in their hands. Most of them are just salespeople who are trying to sell you one of a series of financial products for which they and their company will receive a commission or fee. You can do better.

If you don't know enough to make the decisions yourself, then start learning. Most of what appears complicated is just jargon and terminology that you will be able to master if you apply yourself. At the very minimum, you need to learn enough to be able to distinguish between wise and foolish counsel. It will be your job and your money on the line, so don't let a fear of being a fool cause you pass off critical responsibility onto others who may be less qualified than you think.

Many people don't follow their dreams. They keep putting them on the back burner for safer times. In this way, they end up 10 or 20 years later still not having started that new business or not working in a career they want. They let the advice of others convince them to wait for the appropriate time for changing careers or starting down the path to their own business.

Don't be afraid. You can do it.

More and more people are finding themselves pursuing their own career as their only option after a major layoff. You might as well start getting ready so that if this happens to you, you will be able to pursue a business you know and enjoy.

You may not be able to do it using the luxury plan, but there are many ways to gain entry into a new career besides the ones that cost lots of money. If you really want to do something, you must overcome the fear of failure. The best way I know for how to do this is by failing a few times. This lets you know that failure is not such a horrible thing. You will learn from each failure and be better prepared for future success.

Remain Flexible

Remaining flexible in the context of personal risk management has two components: keeping a diverse set of skills so that you can find another job easily should your job or business venture not work out and keeping flexible investments by diversifying and keeping some liquid assets.

The best Silicon Valley engineers present a good model of how to maintain flexibility in job skills. They are constantly trying out new technologies, working on side projects, and keeping their skills up-to-date. They know that the startup environment in the valley is notoriously volatile and that they might be out of a job on short notice. They also know that there will always be openings for smart people who have current experience with the latest technologies. So they keep sharp, knowing that even in a tough job market they will do fine.

I don't think any type of risk management can be expected to always work, i.e., protect capital from any event. As Rich told us many years ago, you must take some money out of the game every now and then. T-bills, gold, diamonds, real estate (?) are some of the assets that might hold value when all hell breaks loose.

—Jerry Parker

Flexible investments are those that are diversified with a component of liquid assets. Simply put, diversifying is another way of saying, "Don't put all your eggs in one basket." Keeping liquid assets means keeping some of your investment in assets that can be easily converted to cash. A house is not a liquid asset, but a money market or mutual fund investment is. You can pay next month's bills with liquid assets, but not with your house.

In fact, an investment such as a house can be a big anchor around your neck if you lose your job. You will still have to pay your mortgage, and you will have to sell or rent the house if you can't find work nearby and have to move elsewhere. Selling a house in a bad housing market sometimes can take a year or more.

The failure to diversify sufficiently is the single biggest problem I see for most nonprofessionals. They keep too much of their net worth tied up in one or two investments. For those with a home, that home may represent 80 to 90 percent of their net worth. This makes them very vulnerable to a downturn in the housing market. Others may have all their money invested in their company's stock through a company-sponsored 401(k) program. This leaves them vulnerable to problems with their company. If that company hits hard times, an individual might end up facing the loss of both job and fortune at the same time. This is bad risk management.

Remaining flexible also means keeping some cash reserve. If you lose a job or an unexpected illness strikes, cash in the bank will get you through those troubled times. Cash invested in real estate won't. So don't spend all your cash to put 20 percent down on a house if you won't have any left over. You are better off putting 10 percent down and then keeping the other money tucked away in case you need it. The extra 10 percent in your down payment will not help you to pay the bills in the event of a problem. Even better, perhaps, would be to buy a less expensive house so that you can afford a down payment and a reserve for emergencies. This is the option that leaves you with the greatest flexibility.

Focus on Decisions, Not Outcomes

The most important factor for managing risk on a personal level is to focus on decisions, not outcomes. Don't play Monday morning quarterback with your own decisions.

If you lose a lot of money in the stock market, that doesn't mean you shouldn't ever invest again. If you make money buying a stock, that doesn't mean buying it was a good decision.

Remember, analyze your decisions based on the information you had available at the time you made that decision. If you learned something new, that's great. Just don't berate yourself for making a decision based on information you didn't have when you made that decision. This is easier said than done but it is important.

Risking Builds Confidence

Risk and uncertainty are a given. They are all around you, and some are unavoidable. Learn to respect those unavoidable risks. But don't be afraid of risk. It can be harnessed for good or bad.

The only way to build the confidence that is required for success is by taking risks. Each risk, whether it results in good or bad, will result in a learning experience. You will learn what works and what doesn't. Even risks that result in a bad outcome will build confidence and make future risks easier.

When you take risks, you will learn that failure is not so scary. You will learn that success is not always the best teacher. Most of all, though, you will learn how to better be yourself.

DREAMING BIGGER DREAMS

There is nothing like a dream to create the future.
—Victor Hugo

I remember as a young child of five when the first lunar module landed on the moon. I did not at the time understand just how big a step Neil Armstrong took on that day, July 20, 1969. I did not understand the terror that *Sputnik* had cast over America, nor that it had been just over eight years prior, on July 25, 1961, when President John F. Kennedy had challenged Congress:

> *I believe that this nation should commit itself to achieving the goal, before this decade is out, of landing a man on the moon and returning him safely to the Earth.*

As I grew up, I naturally expected more of the same. I expected that we would soon go to Mars and beyond. In the mid-1970s we had *Skylab*—a 100-ton orbiting space station in which astronauts stayed for weeks or months running experiments. Then, in the early 1980s, we launched the space shuttle, a partially reusable "advanced" space vehicle that returns to the Earth like a glider.

Since that time, we have done relatively little. Our space exploration has crawled by comparison to the 1960s when NASA was in its infancy. What happened?

I remember as a small child learning about poverty and starvation and thinking that eventually we would solve these problems as technology brought better growing methods to poor countries. I was optimistic about the future because the country was optimistic.

Something has happened in the last 30 to 40 years to change that. We seem to have lost our faith in our ability to deliver on our dreams.

We have even stopped dreaming big dreams. We have stopped thinking about how the future could be different in big ways. In the process and along the way, we have lost much of our ability to make it better in small ways. Part of the reason we settle for this lack of progress is because we have seen a lot of money and time spent in the pursuit of these noble goals. So after decades of almost no progress, we have grown tired of trying. We have come to believe that our dreams are not possible, that we have been unrealistic.

I don't agree with this kind of thinking. In fact, I posit that it is our very belief that some of our dreams are so big and hard to accomplish that has kept them so far away. It has kept us from demanding more from ourselves and our government. Consider one specific example: advanced transportation.

Rethinking Transportation

Anyone who follows trends can see that the U.S. model for a transportation system based primarily on cars is not sustainable. Cars are inefficient compared with many other forms of transportation.

Yet the automobile serves as a symbol of status and prosperity. So developing nations, in an effort to "modernize," have been following our lead in developing a car-based infrastructure. But cars are starting to choke the developing world and are threatening to push global warming over the edge at the worst possible time.

Many countries see the ill-effects of following the U.S. model for transportation development with its cars and highways. The pollution of China's major cities is one example. According to a May 2008 report by the World Watch Institute, 16 of the world's most polluted cities are in China. Automobiles cause a large portion of the pollution in these Chinese cities. This is one of the reasons that the Chinese government banned automobile use every other day during the 2008 Beijing Olympics. This ban, combined with a shutdown of the 100 worst polluting factories, resulted in the best air quality in over a decade during the Olympics.

Cars are also very unsafe. In the United States alone, over 40,000 people die each year in auto accidents. The equivalent of more than 10 times the number of people killed in the September 11 attacks die every year because of auto accidents. Additional hundreds of thousands are injured and maimed in these accidents every year.

Traffic and time spent driving cost many additional lifetimes. According to the Texas Transportation Institute's 2007 *Urban Mobility Report*, traffic congestion in American cities costs $78 billion in the form of 4.2 billion lost hours, or the equivalent of more than 6,000 lifetimes, spent waiting in traffic. It also wastes 2.9 billion gallons of fuel, or more than 58 fully loaded supertankers.

Advanced transportation systems could easily eliminate the problems with automobiles, especially in developing countries that do not have huge established infrastructure. The technology to safely automate driving and eliminate accidents has existed for several decades. Higher-speed transport without traffic is possible. Fuel economy in the equivalent range of 200 to 300 mpg is possible today. But we need to completely rethink our transportation systems.

The solutions proposed by our government are typical incremental extensions to our existing system. More buses, extensions to public transit systems, hybrid and plug-in electric cars, and others. Buses and public transit solutions represent, at best, minor improvements in speed, fuel efficiency, and safety. Hybrid and plug-in electric cars represent significant improvements in efficiency but without any improvements in safety or travel times. We can do much better.

Finally, for long-distance travel, we have built a system that is almost entirely based on airports and airplanes, even for cities that are as little as 200 miles apart. While Europe has high-speed rail systems that connect most major cities, the United States does not.

To make anything other than minor improvements, we would do well to think about what we would like to have if we could start over again and didn't have to think about our existing infrastructure. Ideally, we'd like the benefits of cars without any of the downsides. This is possible. Existing technology can support an energy-efficient high-speed transportation system that eliminates the possibility for vehicle collisions and traffic jams using automated guidance and advanced highway infrastructure.

So the question remains: Why haven't we seen progress here? If the new ideas are so good, why aren't there cities with advanced transportation already up and running? Why haven't we at least started?

Cities, Progress, and Risk

The reason we haven't seen many advances in transportation is because of the risk aversion in the decision-making process and among the decision makers for our cities.

For most cities, any new transportation system requires the combined decision of the city itself and its associated regional transit authority. For a single city, there is generally a metropolitan transportation board that makes transit decisions. In the San Francisco Bay area, it is Bay Area Regional Transit (BART). In Chicago, it is the Regional Transit Authority(RTA), which is a combination of the Chicago Transit Authority, the Metra commuter rail system, and the PACE suburban bus systems, for example.

Committees shun risk.

So what comes out of these committees are low-risk incremental improvements, projects that have worked in other cities, projects that are extensions of existing transit systems. Committees discard the newer ideas because they are untried and the companies that market them are generally smaller companies with few, if any, existing customers. So, for a particular city, choosing an advanced transportation system represents a very high-risk decision; too high.

The problem of advanced transportation is a perfect example of an area where the federal government can act to break the risk deadlock. It may not make sense for a given city to take on the risk of a new technology, but it definitely makes sense for the country as a whole to take the risk. This is especially true if we want to revive the rust-belt cities like Detroit, Cleveland, and Toledo. New transportation technologies and standards could return the United States to dominance in transportation.

Competition and Standards

The Internet became such a big success because it defined a standard way for networks to connect with each other and for computers to talk to other computers even if they existed in different networks. The standardization of railroad rails, cars, and coupling hardware greatly increased the efficiency of rail shipping. The adoption of a standard-sized shipping container revolutionized the cargo shipping business because it greatly reduced the cost of door-to-door shipping.

Similarly, a new advanced transportation technology standard could revolutionize transport. Standards could make it possible for many different companies to build parts of the system. Standards could make it possible for smaller companies to build parts of the system. Standards could make it possible for us to more easily improve the system in the future. Standards would make it possible for public and private transport to share the same infrastructure like busses do on today's streets and highways.

So the task then is to determine what the standard should be. What should this new transportation system look like? What capabilities should it have? What constraints?

Since none of us have "the answer" to these questions, and there is no "correct" answer, we need to learn. The quickest way for us to learn as a society is for us to adopt an evolutionary model. We should run five or six diverse experiments and then quickly adapt from these new experiments to arrive at a solution. For example, the federal government could agree to fund advanced transportation pilot projects in five or six major cities. These new projects would serve to implement public transportation for these cities and would also be used as experiments. The best ideas could be combined into a new national infrastructure standard that would serve as the basis for new vehicles and highways.

We need to encourage investment in new transportation technologies by ensuring that there will be a market for those technologies. By investing in advanced transportation technologies, the U.S. government will ensure that our transportation industry is at the fore of twenty-first-century transportation development. The large market assured by government investment will, in turn, attract venture capital investment. A little new investment now could mean hundreds of billions of dollars of revenue over the next few decades as we replace our aging infrastructure with a newer and better one.

It *does not make sense to rebuild and replace* the crumbling infrastructure that America built in the 1950s. We should use the poor state of our highways and bridges as an opportunity to replace them with something better. The same companies that now install bridges and highway overpasses can do the same with those designed for a new type of highway. The same vehicle manufacturers that are now struggling against foreign competition could provide the vehicles and electric propulsion systems that power a new transportation infrastructure. If we lead in innovation, our transportation industry will lead, too. If we wait, our transportation industry will continue to wither.

When we don't know what will work, we should experiment, and we should experiment with as much diversity as possible. In other words, we should try lots of ideas, and the ideas should be as different from each other as possible. We should fund the projects of more mad scientists and fewer rational ones. We should implement more bottom-up research and less top-down research.

If you think this is asking too much, I ask you to first consider whether it compares to the pace and effort required to send men to the moon in 1969. If we could build a space program from the ground up and go to the moon in just over ten years, then we can certainly redesign our transportation system in as many years.

Finally

In these times of great uncertainty, we as a society need to become more adaptable and flexible. We can do this if we follow the seven rules for mastering risk. These rules can serve as a practical framework for managing the increasing uncertainty of the modern world.

We need to behave humbly and we need to face the reality of our current circumstances. The seven rules are no panacea. I do not offer them as such. Instead, they represent a series of principles and ideas that have proven effective in many domains where risk and uncertainty are highest. These principles can serve to help us through the difficult times ahead but we must first apply them.

We collectively stand at a time of crisis on many different fronts: economic, social, as well as environmental. The world economy is reeling from too much consumption and reliance on a glut of easy credit. Society is still trying to come to grips with the implications of globalization of culture and politics in an era where technology makes it possible for a small group of fanatics to kill and maim thousands. The requirements for addressing global warming, reducing consumption and increasing investment in alternatives are not practical for the developing world. The developed countries like the United States must therefore bear the greatest burden in our research to find technologies that developing nations can afford.

Each of these crises increases the uncertainty in the world.

So we cannot afford more of the same in our government or in the way we work together. We need to take more risks, but we need to do so with a healthy respect for reality. The seven rules offer an excellent framework for doing so.

Most of all, though, we must dream big dreams again. We must believe in those dreams. Only by doing this will we live up to our potential.

INDEX

ABOUT THE AUTHOR

Curtis Faith is the author of the bestselling *Way of the Turtle*. In his early twenties, Faith earned more than $30 million as a member of the Chicago trading group, the Turtles. He founded several software and high-tech startups, including a public and an Inc. 500 company.